Macau

WORLD BIBLIOGRAPHICAL SERIES

General Editors:
Robert G. Neville (Executive Editor)
John J. Horton   Ian Wallace
Hans H. Wellisch   Ralph Lee Woodward, Jr.

John J. Horton is Deputy Librarian of the University of Bradford and currently Chairman of its Academic Board of Studies in Social Sciences. He has maintained a longstanding interest in the discipline of area studies and its associated bibliographical problems, with special reference to European Studies. In particular he has published in the field of Icelandic and of Yugoslav studies, including the two relevant volumes in the World Bibliographical Series.

Ian Wallace is Professor of Modern Languages at Loughborough University of Technology. A graduate of Oxford in French and German, he also studied in Tübingen, Heidelberg and Lausanne before taking teaching posts at universities in the USA, Scotland and England. He specializes in East German affairs, especially literature and culture, on which he has published numerous articles and books. In 1979 he founded the journal *GDR Monitor*, which he continues to edit.

Hans H. Wellisch is Professor emeritus at the College of Library and Information Services, University of Maryland. He was President of the American Society of Indexers and was a member of the International Federation for Documentation. He is the author of numerous articles and several books on indexing and abstracting, and has published *The Conversion of Scripts* and *Indexing and Abstracting: an International Bibliography*. He also contributes frequently to *Journal of the American Society for Information Science, The Indexer* and other professional journals.

Ralph Lee Woodward, Jr. is Chairman of the Department of History at Tulane University, New Orleans, where he has been Professor of History since 1970. He is the author of *Central America, a Nation Divided*, 2nd ed. (1985), as well as several monographs and more than sixty scholarly articles on modern Latin America. He has also compiled volumes in the World Bibliographical Series on *Belize* (1980), *Nicaragua* (1983), and *El Salvador* (1988). Dr. Woodward edited the Central American section of the *Research Guide to Central America and the Caribbean* (1985) and is currently editor of the Central American history section of the *Handbook of Latin American Studies*.

VOLUME 105

Macau

Richard Louis Edmonds

Compiler

CLIO PRESS

OXFORD, ENGLAND · SANTA BARBARA, CALIFORNIA
DENVER, COLORADO

British Library Cataloguing in Publication Data

Edmonds, Richard Louis 1948—
Macau. — (World bibliographical series; v.105).
I. Macau. Bibliographies
I. Title   II. Series
016.951'26

ISBN 1–85109–090–8

Clio Press Ltd.,
55 St. Thomas' Street,
Oxford OX1 1JG, England.

ABC-CLIO,
130 Cremona Drive,
Santa Barbara,
CA 93117, USA.

Designed by Bernard Crossland.
Typeset by Columns Design and Production Services, Reading, England.
Printed and bound in Great Britain by
Billing and Sons Ltd., Worcester.

THE WORLD BIBLIOGRAPHICAL SERIES

This series, which is principally designed for the English speaker, will eventually cover every country in the world, each in a separate volume comprising annotated entries on works dealing with its history, geography, economy and politics; and with its people, their culture, customs, religion and social organization. Attention will also be paid to current living conditions – housing, education, newspapers, clothing, etc.– that are all too often ignored in standard bibliographies; and to those particular aspects relevant to individual countries. Each volume seeks to achieve, by use of careful selectivity and critical assessment of the literature, an expression of the country and an appreciation of its nature and national aspirations, to guide the reader towards an understanding of its importance. The keynote of the series is to provide, in a uniform format, an interpretation of each country that will express its culture, its place in the world, and the qualities and background that make it unique. The views expressed in individual volumes, however, are not necessarily those of the publisher.

VOLUMES IN THE SERIES

To my
mother and father

Contents

Contents

Contents

Preface

The purpose of the Macau volume is to present an annotated list of books on Macau which will help English-speaking readers to study aspects of the territory. With its large Chinese ethnic population and long history of Portuguese administration, Macau possesses a rich historical heritage in Chinese and, particularly, in Portuguese. References to the territory in English are numerous, considering the small size of Macau, and this bibliography includes almost all available English and French references as well as a considerable number of Portuguese items. The Chinese references are more selective. It has always been my feeling that one must read the local literature to study a place and this bibliography indicates just how important this is in the case of Macau.

This bibliography is not comprehensive but selective. The small size of the territory, however, has allowed me to go into much more detail than that found in many of the other bibliographies in the series. In addition, the small Portuguese readership in Macau means that many books are printed in runs of only 500 to 2000 copies and, as a consequence, the availability of books in British libraries is restricted. Although the reader may well have trouble finding some of these materials in the smaller cities of the English speaking world, the vast majority can be found in the British Library or the School of Oriental and African Studies Library in London.

Since Macau played a key rôle in the transmission of culture between the East and West and was the cornerstone of Portugal's trade with East Asia, particularly during the 16th and 17th centuries, some works on the Portuguese in East Asia have also been included.

Full names have been given for authors when they are known. Portuguese names and book titles follow the orthography of the work in question while all other Portuguese words follow modern orthography. Chinese names pose more of a problem. In cases of proper names specific to Macau, names are romanized in the local language, Cantonese, following the romanization used in the *Dicionário Chinês-Português* (q.v.). For the titles of Chinese books

Preface

published in Macau, Cantonese romanization is followed by the Standard Chinese (Mandarin) *pinyin* romanization in brackets. Words and proper nouns referring to China and to books published in China are written in *pinyin* romanization only. Names of people and italicized Chinese words given in *pinyin* include tone marks whereas place names do not. Chinese and Japanese names are given in the bibliography with the surname first.

As Macau is a relatively little-known territory, the introduction to this volume aims to provide a wide-ranging overview of Macau, its geography, history, peoples and unique character. Names of places and institutions are generally given in Portuguese, as this is the form by which they are best known in Macau, with Cantonese and English versions cited where necessary. Many variant names are clarified in the glossary.

Acknowledgements

Jane Bingham and Robert Neville of Clio Press were encouraging, competent and helpful editors. Charles d'Orban of the Chinese section in the School of Oriental and African Studies Library was kind enough to help in ordering as many books as he possibly could. Assistance in Macau came from Rodolfo Azevedo, Rolf Dieter Cremer, Maria Armanda Rodrigues, Eleanor Smith, and Liz Thomas. I also wish to thank my colleagues, Hugh Baker and Christopher Howe, of the School of Oriental and African Studies, who lent me books to read for inclusion in this bibliography and Catherine Lawrence, who drew the map of Macau for this volume. Last of all, I wish to thank my wife, Mali, and my children, Sarah, Daniel and Mary for being who they are.

Richard Louis Edmonds
Berkhamsted
May 1989

Introduction

Macau was the first port on the China coast to come under the influence of a foreign power and will be the last to return to Chinese sovereignty in 1999. It is also the last Portuguese administered overseas territory. In these ways, Macau is something of an anachronism and has a special place in historical geography. In a period of history when English-speaking nations have come to dominate the West's relations with East Asia, Macau, with its interaction of Chinese and Portuguese cultures, stands out as unique.

The territory has an important rôle to play in the future of China and in East-West relations in general. After 1999, Macau, like Hong Kong from 1997, will become a special economic region of the People's Republic of China. The Chinese hope to maintain the existing capitalist systems in Macau and Hong Kong while incorporating them within the larger Communist state. The success of that venture has important implications for the future relations of mainland China and Taiwan and will be an instructive example of political cohabitation.

Geography

With less than seventeen square kilometres in total, Macau is small, even when compared with neighbouring Hong Kong. The territory is composed of three distinct parts; the Macau peninsula (6.05 sq. km.), and the islands of Taipa (3.779 sq. km.) and Coloane (7.087 sq. km.) to the south. It takes less than one hour to travel by bus from the extreme north of the Macau peninsula to the southern end of Coloane.

Since the 1950s, official statistics of Macau's population have consistently underestimated numbers because of the large proportion of illegal Chinese immigrants. Today, it is stated that the population is around 426,000 although a figure close to 550,000 is probably more accurate.

Macau has a warm, moist climate which is influenced by its coastal location. Prevailing winds follow the monsoonal pattern with winter winds from the north gradually shifting to the east and south during spring and summer.

The peninsula of Macau is composed of outcrops of igneous rocks, including granite, aplite, pegmatite and basalt, intermixed with or covered by sediments. Earthquakes were reported as late as the 1830s, but there has been no recent volcanic activity in Macau.

Macau peninsula

The peninsula of Macau is connected to the People's Republic of China by an isthmus which is only 200 metres wide at the border. It was probably an island until just before the Portuguese arrived in 1557 and there is some speculation that the isthmus was covered with water at high tide when these Europeans first visited Macau.

Today, all land traffic to the People's Republic of China must pass through the Porta do Cerco or Barrier Gate. Constructed in 1870 to replace the 16th-century Chinese-built gate, it is crowned with a quote from Luís Vaz de Camões' epic poem, *Os Lusíadas*, which, roughly translated, reads 'Honour your country for it will look after you'.

Although it covers less than thirty-six per cent of the territory's total area, the peninsula is the core of Macau. Over ninety-nine per cent of the population reside here.

In contrast to the more recently developed landscape of the islands, the peninsula still has some of the character of a traditional city. The mixture of architectural styles makes the city reminiscent of Lisbon in some places and in others of Guangzhou (Canton), although the European style predominates. The sense of a Mediterranean landscape is reinforced by the fact that the city of Macau is spread over seven hills with crooked streets often opening into central squares.

The islands

Taipa Taipa has traditionally been known as a sleepy backwater of Macau which is itself considered a backwater of Hong Kong. All of that has changed rapidly since the 2.56 kilometre long Governador Nobre de Carvalho Bridge, designed by Edgar Cardoso, was built between the peninsula and Taipa in 1974. Initially, a toll was charged but since the tolls were eliminated, access to and from the islands has been facilitated for all except, perhaps, illegal immigrants, since vehicles are often searched on the Taipa side of the bridge.

Although much of the island is undergoing development, Taipa Village displays a street pattern which is close to that found on the Macau peninsula. Without the volume of traffic and hustle and bustle of urban Macau it is a most attractive spot for tourists. Commercial activities in the village are largely restricted to restaurants and markets and industrial firms are local in character, except for the now virtually defunct fireworks factories.

Coloane   Since the completion of the Governador Nobre de Carvalho Bridge in 1974, it has been possible to live in Coloane and commute to the Macau peninsula although surprisingly few people have opted for such a life-style. Coloane Village is similar to Taipa Village although it has a slightly more rural character. In addition to Coloane village, there are several smaller settlements on Coloane, Hác Sá and Ká Hó being two of the more famous.

Land reclamation

Reclamation on Macau began in the late 19th century with the joining of Ilha Verde to the peninsula. Known in early times as Devil's Island, this former islet to the northwest of the peninsula is now connected to Macau by a man-made roadway.

Another major project was the joining of the two parts of the island of Taipa early in the 20th century. Taipa has been linked to the peninsula by a bridge and plans are now underway to reclaim land to the east of the island for Macau's airport.

In 1983, an ambitious plan was announced for Macau and Zhuhai (the Chinese special economic zone to the north of the Macau peninsula) to act jointly in reclaiming 110 hectares of Macau's Porto Exterior for urban development. Another project is planned for industrial development and low-income housing in the Areia Preta, to the northeast of the Macau peninsula. These two projects, plus land reclamation off Taipa for Macau's airport, would double the size of the territory. However, with the exception of the airport, it is unlikely that these reclamations will be started much before 1999.

Urban development

Portuguese settlement was concentrated initially at the foot of the Monte Fortress and confined to an area south of the defensive wall. This four foot thick wall, which was constructed between 1622 and 1629, ran between the Monte Fortress and Guia Hill in the centre of the peninsula, extending to both coasts. With only two gates along its entire length, the wall acted as a restricting element on Portuguese settlement until well into the 19th century.

In the early 20th century, a Spanish architect designed the Bairro de São Lázaro which was the first planned urban project beyond the old wall. Since that time, significant land reclamation to the north of the old defensive wall has caused the population centre of the peninsula to move gradually northeastwards.

Introduction

Current development is concentrated on reclaimed land, some of which, along the Porto Exterior, has sat idle since early in the 20th century. Increasingly, the remaining agricultural land is being urbanized and land due to be reclaimed in the future will undoubtedly be used for urban development. The establishment of the Zhuhai special economic zone to the north of Macau in 1979 and the improvement in Macau-China contacts have both contributed to the inevitable process of urbanization. With such rapid development taking place in Macau, there will soon no longer be idle land on the peninsula.

The urbanization of Macau since the 1970s has put a tremendous amount of pressure on the remaining open spaces. The situation is most serious on the peninsula where the northern part is covered by low-income housing, multi-storey buildings and light industrial plants. Taipa is also urbanizing at an appallingly rapid rate with high-rise housing, hotels and the University occupying what were once paddy- or tree-covered areas. As a consequence, the flora and fauna of the island are under threat.

Tourism is dependent on a healthy and aesthetically pleasing environment and the need to encourage visitors has led to a growing concern for the preservation of historic buildings. In 1976, the Comissão de Defesa do Património Arquitectónico, Paisajístico e Cultural (Committee for the Preservation of Macau's Heritage) was created and was given further powers in 1984. The Committee has close links with the Instituto Cultural de Macau (Macau Cultural Institute). Under its direction, an exhaustive inventory of monuments and buildings is being undertaken and certain areas and buildings have been awarded protected status. One example of conservation in Macau is the plan to convert five early 20th-century Portuguese-style mansions along the water front on the eastern edge of Taipa village into a 'cultural village' (or mân fá ch'ün with a museum (which is already open), a centre for arts and crafts, a gallery and a restaurant.

Harbours and bays

The harbours and bays of Macau have always been vital to the territory, although their pattern of usage has changed and is changing still, due to siltation, the increased tonnage of ships and the development of new harbours.

The Porto Interior, or Inner Harbour, located on the western side of the peninsula, was Macau's major harbour area from the 19th century to the present day. The tea which was eventually dumped in Boston harbour began its journey to America from here. In the 19th century, there were ten wharves in the harbour, approximately four specializing in the Hong Kong service, two in the Guangzhou service,

xviii

and one for the opium monopoly. Nowadays, however, the silting-up of the channels combined with the use of larger ships and the construction of the Porto Exterior, or Outer Harbour, on the eastern side of the peninsula plus the new Ká Hó port on Coloane mean that the Porto Interior is increasingly unimportant, although coastal traffic still goes through customs checks there.

The Porto Exterior, on the peninsula's Hong Kong side, is now the main passenger port with links to both Hong Kong and China. It was enclosed with breakwaters by a Dutch firm between 1923 and 1926, from which time it has gradually grown in importance, especially for passenger ferry services. Freight is not likely to increase as most new freight shipments will be directed to the future port at Ká Hó on Coloane.

The most famous bay in Macau, the Praia Grande or Nám Van, has been the subject of landscape paintings for centuries. Prior to the 19th century, the Praia Grande was the major harbour for trade, but as a result of siltation and the growth in the size of ships, the bulk of trade shifted to the Porto Interior. Today, the harbour is very shallow and a sea wall has been built beside the road although the banyan trees still give the Praia a feeling of the past. The northern part of the harbour was reclaimed when the Hotel Lisboa was built and there are plans to convert the shallow bay into a lake.

The Pâc On Bay on the island of Taipa is now undergoing reclamation. Once the principal harbour for the island, Pâc On is being reclaimed in order to build a waste treatment plant and a jail.

Another harbour on Taipa is the picturesque and quiet Bay of Nossa Senhora da Esperança on the south side of the island. Sealed off by the Taipa-Coloane causeway on one side and now essentially a mud flat at low tide, it is likely that this bay will be reclaimed. Much of the bay supports a mangrove-type plant sometimes known as spiny bears breech (Acanthus Ilicifolius L.). The few vessels stopping at Taipa nowadays use the Ponte No. 1 wharf at the extreme southwest tip of the island.

Ká Hó Bay, on the northeast coast of Coloane, will be the port of the future for Macau. The contract to expand the harbour into a deep water port was signed in 1988 between the Macau government and a consortium of Chinese, Portuguese, and Macau interests.

History

Early history

There is some evidence of settlement on the Macau peninsula at least two centuries before the Portuguese arrived in the mid-16th century. The Má Kók Temple (Măgé Mìu) and the Kun Iam Tong

(Guānyīn Táng) or Temple to the Goddess of Mercy, were both apparently founded in the 13th century. However, Hou Kéng (Háojìng), as Macau was known before the arrival of the Portuguese, was not a major Chinese settlement.

Chinese overseas trade had flourished intermittently from the 7th century onwards, but, by the 16th century, when the Portuguese reached Asia by sea, the Chinese were already practising a closed door policy, in part to minimize contact with pirates who were marauding the China coast. For the Portuguese, on the other hand, the 15th and 16th centuries were periods of ambitious colonial expansion. Following the capture of Ceuta in Morocco during 1415, the Portuguese steadily established control at points along the coasts of Africa and Asia. In 1511, at Malacca (now in Malaysia), they first came into contact with the Chins, whose country they called China, and, by 1521, they were established in the Spice Islands (now part of Indonesia). Although the Spice Islands had been their original goal, the Portuguese were soon attracted by the possibility of trade with the Chins and it was Jorge Álvares, in the company of two other Portuguese, who first set foot on the south China coast in 1513. Many other Portuguese were to follow Álvares' tracks to China.

The Portuguese arrived on the south China coast at an ideal time, since they could fill the trade gap left by the Chinese by acting as middlemen in reviving China's trade with Southeast Asia, South Asia, and eventually Japan. To do this effectively, however, the Portuguese needed a base of operations closer to China than their post at Malacca. Between the years 1552 and 1557, a series of trading posts were created along the China coast, although the Portuguese were forced to abandon each of them in turn before the establishment of Macau around 1557.

Although it is known that the Portuguese visited the Macau area before 1557, it is not clear when they first touched land at Hou Kéng. One author gives a date of 1533, but 1555 is the most common estimate and it was not until after 1557 that the city began to expand rapidly.

The choice of Macau was no doubt influenced by the qualities of its harbours, the Praia Grande and the Porto Interior. Combining good shelter from storms with adequate water depth for the Portuguese carracks, the harbours must also have appeared easy to defend.

Macau as the centre of European activities in East Asia

The period 1560 to 1640 marked Macau's zenith as an economic centre. Indeed, it is no exaggeration to say that Macau at that time was the focus of all trade between East Asia and Western Europe. This rise to economic importance was accomplished within a few decades, aided by the opening of trade to Nagasaki in Japan during 1570 and the development of the Manila (Philippines) trade from the late 16th century. However, Macau was to decline almost as abruptly as it had risen, albeit with a very long tailing off after the initial slump.

During this period the Portuguese were the only Europeans to have extensive contact with the Chinese. Although the peninsula was divided from mainland China by a wall constructed by the Chinese in 1573, access was possible via a gate in the wall which was opened once every five days. In 1621, the city of Macau presented three cannon to the Míng emperor and in 1629 the Míng sent a mission to Macau to buy more. Ten guns were presented to the Míng court along with some gunners and the Jesuit Father João Rodrigues (1561-1634) as their interpreter.

Throughout the 16th and early 17th centuries, Macau was an important Catholic mission centre. Missionaries from all over Europe used the territory as their East Asia base.

Macau's decline and brief revival

Macau's rapid initial decline can be attributed to several causes. The union of the crown with Castile from 1580-1640 put Portugal into conflict with Spain's enemies and, according to many Portuguese historians, led to the drain of Portugal's resources to finance Spain's ambitions. One result of this union was a strain in the Macau-Manila trade.

Coinciding with Portugal's weakening, the rise of the Dutch to dominance in East Asian trade seriously damaged Macau. In 1622, a Dutch force attacked Macau but was repulsed by the explosion of a Dutch gunpowder wagon and by an unlikely band of Portuguese soliders, drunken negro slaves, Macaense citizens and priests.

The expulsion of the Portuguese from Japan in 1639, because of suspected complicity in the Shimabara Revolt, brought an end to Macau's links with Nagasaki and other Japanese ports. Already, by 1639, the volume of Portuguese trade with the Japanese was far smaller than that of the Chinese and the Dutch and, in 1641, the Dutch captured Malacca which cut Macau off from Goa (the capital of Portuguese India) for a time. In the long run, this meant that Macau became even more isolated than before from the rest of the Portuguese empire.

In 1717, European companies were permitted to set up trading 'factories' in Guangzhou and the Chinese reintroduced the regulation whereby all direct trade between Europeans and Chinese had to go through the Portuguese. Although this order only lasted until 1723, it brought a brief period of prosperity to Macau.

Macau's continued stagnation

In general, prosperity eluded the city although it did manage to maintain a significant trading rôle up until the founding of Hong Kong in 1841. Although Macau's rôle as an intermediary between the Europeans and the Chinese ceased in 1723, the peninsula still provided a useful trading base for foreign merchants. From 1764, English, French and other foreigners found that they could remain in the territory by obtaining Portuguese nationality and permission to reside in Macau from Goa. Gradually, British, Parsees, Armenians, Dutch, French, and others began to take up residence, often operating in cooperation with local Portuguese merchants. From this time onwards, the British or, more appropriately, the East India Company, became prominent in the city and Macau was the first place on the China coast to have an English-language newspaper.

Attempted invasions of Macau

During the early 19th century, Macau was twice almost invaded by the British. In 1802, Britain assumed that Portugal had concluded peace with France in the previous year and attempted invasion while, in 1808, Macau was again occupied by British troops who quickly departed when the Portuguese got the Chinese to intervene on their behalf and threaten British trade at Guangzhou. However, it was the Chinese Commissioner, Lín Zéxú, who actually entered Macau in 1839 as China attempted to show her authority during the opium crisis.

Macau languished after the rise of Hong Kong in 1841, over-shadowed by the supremacy of the British Empire and the new colony's superior harbour. In 1843, the Portuguese attempted, with limited success, to obtain formal concession of Macau and, in 1844, the territory was separated from Goa and combined with Timor and Solor (now in Indonesia) as a Portuguese 'province'.

Britain threatened Portuguese sovereignty again in 1849 when a party of marines was landed to rescue one determined Protestant, James Summers, who had refused to doff his hat for a Catholic procession on the feast of Corpus Christi. The Governor, João Ferreira do Amaral, protested to the British who justified their action on the grounds that Macau was part of China and therefore the British had extraterritorial rights. The Chinese saw this as a chance to get rid of the Portuguese and murdered Amaral. Three days later, on 22 August 1849, the Chinese opened fire on Portuguese troops at the Porta do Cerco. A young Macaense colonel, Vicente Nicolau de Mesquita, accompanied by some thirty-two men, stormed the Chinese fort at Baishaling (Passaleão) which was defended by 400 soldiers, blew up the magazine and reaffirmed Portuguese control of the city.

Oddly enough, Portugal was not to obtain recognition of its sovereignty over Macau until the Treaty of Tianjin in 1862. Article two of this treaty stated that China granted perpetual occupation and administration of Macau and its dependencies to Portugal as a Portuguese possession. A protocol was signed in Lisbon in 1887 and was reconfirmed within a Luso-Chinese commercial treaty of 1888. The Nationalist Chinese revoked these treaties in 1928 along with other treaties negotiated with the Western powers which were considered to have been imposed on China. However, Portugal soon negotiated a new accord.

By the early 1900s, Macau's population had reached around 75,000 but instability in China meant that this figure had doubled by the 1930s. By the 1920s, most of the Portuguese in Macau were government and military officials or ecclesiastics, with only a handful of genuine Portuguese merchants remaining in the colony.

World War II

Portugal's neutrality during World War II made Macau a haven for the Chinese, the British and others fleeing the Japanese. After 1937, Chinese immigrants began to arrive in large numbers with the population swelling to about 600,000 after the occupation of Shanghai and Hong Kong. This was a very interesting period in Macau's history as the city was full of spies and was constantly bullied by the surrounding Japanese military presence. The Japanese demanded that the Macau authorities recognize their local 'puppet' government in Guangdong province and the Portuguese were forced to remove their troops from the island of Wanzhai and to allow the Japanese the right of house-to-house search in the territory.

Post-World War II Macau

With the end of World War II, Macau's population dropped and a pattern of emigration, even for the Macaense, began. By 1945, it was clear that the Nationalists wished to get the Portuguese out of Macau but little was done, especially after civil war broke out in China and the British reoccupied Hong Kong. At this time, many people moved to Hong Kong, where Macaense clerks in banks became the norm in the early 1950s. With the Communist takeover of Guangdong in 1949-50, Macau again provided a home for many Chinese immigrants.

During the Korean War, Macau was used as a smuggling point for raw materials and munitions into China and the People's Republic soon realized that Macau had more value as a Portuguese colony than as an integral part of China. However, relations with China were not always good as pressure was put on Lisbon to stop the smuggling of goods. Clashes occurred along the border on two occasions in July 1952 and food supplies were cut off for almost a month.

Despite the state of non-recognition between Portugal and the People's Republic of China, a system evolved whereby Chinese influence was exercised through local Cantonese businessmen. This system, which has operated successfully throughout the post-war period, can still be seen today.

The late 1950s and early 1960s were a relatively peaceful time in Portugal-Macau-China relations with a steady flow of Chinese immigrants arriving in the colony and an estimated seventy-five per cent of these people emigrating again to Hong Kong. Besides the continuous but decreasing trade in smuggled goods to China, items such as Chinese cigarettes began to be smuggled into Hong Kong via Macau.

The Indian takeover of Portuguese Goa, Damão, and Diu in 1961 must have left many people in Macau wondering how long Portugal would hold on to the territory. Although Chinese propaganda against the Portuguese had always been rather tame, the People's Republic expressed support for India's takeover of Goa, so adding fuel to the worries of many in Macau and Lisbon. In 1965, the Nationalist Chinese Commissioner in Macau was withdrawn at the request of the Portuguese, but problems with the Communist régime were not avoided by this move and came to a head during the Cultural Revolution in 1966 with violent anti-government demonstrations by pro-Communist Chinese residents in Macau.

Anti-government demonstrations 1966–67

The anti-government violence of this period was the result of an incident involving land use rights on Taipa. A pro-Communist *kái fóng* (neighbourhood) association applied to demolish some old buildings and build a primary school in their place. The authorities delayed approval of the application, perhaps because the current Governor had been recalled to Lisbon and not replaced. The *kái fóng* association went ahead and began demolition without permission from the Public Works Bureau. On 15 November 1966, police tried to halt work on the site. The 100-odd labourers threatened to beat up the police, riot police were sent in, at least five people were arrested and injuries were sustained on both sides. The next day, the Taipa *kái fóng* association made five demands: that local authorities be dismissed; that the government of Macau make a public apology; that police truncheons be burnt; that compensation be paid to those injured and that there be no repeat of this sort of assault. The Macau authorities did nothing about these demands, again perhaps because there was no Governor.

A fortnight later, workers, schoolchildren and others invaded Government House shouting quotations from the Thoughts of Chairman Máo Zédōng and reiterating the Taipa demands. The new Governor, Nobre de Carvalho, announced on 2 December that the government would establish an inquiry into the Taipa incident. Despite this conciliatory effort, on 3 December eight people were killed and 123 (Macau government figure) to 225 (Macau Trade Union Federation figure) were injured by police and by resident Chinese in serious rioting. In addition, sixty-one arrests were made that day. The library in the Leal Senado and the Santa Casa da Misericórdia were ransacked while the statue honouring the 19th-century Macaense hero, Colonel Vicente Nicolau de Mesquita, was knocked down.

The government immediately backed down and announced it was willing to make the concessions demanded by the pro-Communist groups. The appearance of Chinese gunboats off-shore and in the Porto Interior made the Portuguese even more nervous. However, there were problems with details of the concessions as the Macau government did not wish to refer to its police as murderers, criminals and assassins. By 10 December, the People's Republic became directly involved by making their own demands to the Macau Government. The Portuguese, demoralized by the situation, told Beijing (Peking) that they were pulling out of Macau. The Communists immediately stopped their anti-Portuguese activities after Lisbon had played this last card although minor demonstrations, mostly by local students, continued throughout 1967. The Macau authorities raised a loan from local sources to pay compensation, some of which went to China as well as to local organizations and individuals. On 29 January 1967, the Governor signed an agreement which apologized for police actions and promised compensation as well as banning anti-Communist and pro-Nationalist organizations in Macau and sending back refugees to China.

It is difficult to pin-point the groups behind these anti-Portuguese incidents. The most common assumption is that the Chinese Communists instigated these incidents to embarrass the Portuguese. One alternative idea is that the local left-wing Chinese Chamber of Commerce encouraged the disturbances in order to give themselves a purer political image with the Beijing authorities. There is always the possibility that the riots were what they were said to be by the local left: the protests of a concerned left-wing youth, with the Portuguese police brutality acting as a catalyst for violence. The triads (Chinese secret societies engaged in crime) may have been involved also, since over 100 known members were detained by the police following the riots.

Introduction

Macau and China

From the late 1960s, Portuguese authority in Macau weakened and Beijing had a far stronger say in this 'Portuguese occupied territory' than was indicated by Chinese propaganda of the late 1960s and 1970s. In the months immediately following the January 1967 settlement, the Macau authorities were afraid to enforce laws for fear of political implications, but gradually the government reasserted some of its former authority.

Following the 1974 25 de Abril *coup d'état* in Portugal, the Portuguese government apparently informed the People's Republic of China of its intention to turn the administration of Macau over to China. China refused to discuss the issue and the Portuguese revolutionaries did not feel that there was a case for granting independence. Diplomatic relations were established between Portugal and the People's Republic of China during 1979 and a secret arrangement was worked out whereby Macau was recognized as Chinese territory under Portuguese administration.

In 1984, the Governor, Vasco Almeida e Costa, requested that the Legislative Assembly be dissolved and elections be held in which ethnic Chinese were allowed to vote regardless of their length of residence in Macau. This led to a situation where the Legislative Assembly became dominated by ethnic Chinese for the first time.

When Portuguese President Eanes visited Beijing in 1985 it was announced that Portugal and the People's Republic of China would hold talks about Macau's future and, in March 1987, Macau's fate was decided by a joint Sino-Portuguese declaration signed after the fourth round of talks. The current status will be maintained until 20 December 1999 when administration of Macau will be taken over by the People's Republic of China. Since 1987, there has been a substantial increase in the number of Portuguese residents in Macau, presumably to make a last attempt to lusify the territory and to take advantage of recently planned infrastructural investment.

Political and legislative system

History

Macau's political system is unique in that it has developed through the ongoing relationship between Portugal and China begun four centuries ago. In the early years of settlement, Macau was governed by the Portuguese while the Chinese maintained a customs house in the town and received dues on for all goods imported. Customs were controlled by a Chinese magistrate, residing just north of the city, who was considered by the Chinese to have authority over the Portuguese. In fact, this mandarin controlled the Chinese while the Portuguese paid him ground rent. The Portuguese official in charge of the settlement was the Captain-Major (Capitão-mor) of the Japan voyage who undertook a fixed term of voyages from Portugal or Goa to Macau and on to Japan.

The official ruling senate in Macau, the Senado da Camara (later known as the Leal Senado) dates from 1583. By 1586, the senate had received rights to govern Macau as a city via a viceregal decree signed in Goa and the Captain-Major's control of local affairs was limited to the garrison. (By the early 17th century, the Captain-Major had been replaced by a Captain-General and this post in turn evolved into that of the Governor of Macau.)

With the recognition of Portuguese sovereignty over Macau in 1887, the legal system of Macau began to undergo a process of amalgamation. As in other Portuguese possessions, the territory's laws were integrated into those of Portugal and this process continued until the 1970s. The anti-government riots in Macau during 1966 and 1967, spurred on by the Cultural Revolution in China and the 25 de Abril *coup d'état* in Portugal during 1974, all helped to begin the reversal of colonial integration.

Decentralization, sinification and independence Decentralization was formally implemented in 1976 with a constitutional recognition of Macau's autonomous status. The sinification of Macau's political system began in 1979 when China and Portugal concluded a secret agreement defining Macau as a Chinese territory under Portuguese administration. From 1980 to 1985, the trend was to leave the legal status of the territory unaltered and to maintain stability without any moves towards greater participation in the political system by the local Chinese population. Such a policy was followed more at the request of the People's Republic of China than as the result of any desire on the Portuguese side.

Following the start of negotiations in 1986 for the return of Macau to China, a sinification policy has begun in Macau. This involves increasing the number of locally trained officials and giving the Cantonese language equal status with Portuguese. However, moves towards democratic reform are still not being encouraged.

The promulgation of the Estatuto Orgânico de Macau (Macau Organic Statute) in February 1976 can be taken as the turning-point in Macau's constitutional make-up as this Statute gave the territory great political autonomy. In fact, the Statute can be seen as Macau's constitution since it lays down fundamental principles for adminis-

Introduction

tering the territory. The Portuguese constitution of 1976 stated in article 5(1) that Macau was not part of Portuguese territory and in article 5(4) that Macau was under Portuguese administration. Therefore, in some ways, the Portuguese pre-empted the secret Luso-Chinese agreement of 1979 concerning Macau.

Current political and legislative system

The Macau Assembleia Legislativa (Láp Fát Wui) is composed of seventeen deputies with four-year tenures of office. Only six of these deputies, however, are elected by direct universal suffrage.

In October 1988, elections were held for the six directly elected seats. The turnout of 29.65 per cent of the voters revealed a considerable lack of interest in the political process as it is now constituted. Nonetheless, a more liberal group, the Associação de Amizade Alexandre Ho, increased its number of seats to three at the expense of the pro-Beijing and Macaense business community's União Eleitoral, which retained the other three seats. In addition, six representatives were elected by indirect suffrage.

Five deputies are appointed by the Governor and six are nominated by local civic associations. This shows how the Portuguese and the Chinese business and civic organizations maintain control over the legislature. The law-making process itself is extremely complex and non-democratic, as both Portuguese and Macau bodies possess legislative power over the territory. In general, where there is no exclusive law created in Macau, Portuguese law prevails.

The judicial system of Macau remains subservient to the Portuguese courts since Portuguese higher courts hear appeals against decisions made by the Governor and other high-ranking members of the Macau government. There are three courts or tribunals: the Tribunal da Comarca, the Tribunal Administrativo and the Tribunal Militar. The Tribunal da Comarca is further subdivided into three independent courts. All these are first level courts within the Lisbon judicial district. Gradually, most of Macau's laws are being translated into Chinese.

The highest ranking executive in the Macau government, the Governor, is appointed by the President of the Republic of Portugal and can also be dismissed by the President. Although the Governor does have veto powers over the Legislative Assembly his veto can be overridden by a two-thirds majority vote. Decisions concerning Macau's external affairs still rest with the Portuguese President although it is at the President's discretion to delegate this authority to the Governor of Macau and Presidents have done so in matters strictly concerning Macau.

The Governor is assisted by a support structure of five adjunct secretaries with responsibilities for administration, economics, finance and tourism, public works, education and culture, and social affairs. The Governor is also advised by a Conselho Consultivo or Consultative Council (Chi Sôn Wui) with ten members, half of whom are indirectly elected. In the Consultative Council as well as the Legislative Assembly, the Chinese language (Cantonese) now has official status along with Portuguese. At the ground level are various departments, autonomous bodies and contracted private companies.

Local government is divided into two districts: the Câmara Municipal or Municipal Council (Si Chêng T'éng) with jurisdiction over the Macau peninsula, and the Câmara Municipal das Ilhas or Islands' Municipal Council (Hói Tou Si Chêng T'éng) which administers Taipa and Coloane. The Councils generally administer local affairs such as the management of car parks, public gardens, cemeteries and hawkers.

Civil servants in Macau number close to 8,500 with over eighty-five per cent locals. The remainder include officials recruited from Portugal for fixed periods, largely in the higher echelons of the service. The Macau government has made no attempt to internationalize its civil service by hiring Portuguese-speaking foreigners as the British have done by employing a limited number of Commonwealth and American nationals in Hong Kong. However, the Macau government is now undertaking a major effort to make the majority of its civil servants bilingual in Portuguese and Cantonese.

The people of Macau

The Macaense: the people made by Macau

The Macaense, or as they are sometimes referred to in English, Macanese, are difficult to define either racially or culturally. Most people think of the Macaense as the mixed offspring of the Chinese and Portuguese although some of the old family Macaense say that 'pure' Macaense are a mixture of Portuguese and Malay peoples or combinations of these groups with some African or Japanese blood. At the other end of the spectrum, there are those who say that anyone, or at least any non-Chinese, born in Macau is Macaense. Today, however, most people consider anyone of mixed ancestry who speaks Portuguese, or preferably Portuguese with a Macau accent, as a Macaense.

It is difficult to say how many Macaense there are since their identity is somewhat vague and statistics divide people into Portuguese, Chinese and foreigner categories with the Macaense largely included in the Portuguese category. The tendency is for the Macaense to identify more with Portugal than with China, as one would expect in a colonial situation.

The common pattern of intermarriage in Macau is for Portuguese men to marry Chinese women. In a male-dominated society, this pattern helps to reinforce a stronger Portuguese identity while ensuring a significant Chinese cultural background. The descendants of these marriages are now considered to be part of the Macaense community. New blood is essential if the group is to maintain its identity as there has been significant emigration of Macaense in the past to Shanghai, Hong Kong, and other treaty ports to seek professional or clerical work. No doubt there will be more emigration of Macaense prior to 1999.

Lingu Maquista   Known in the dialect as lingu Maquista or Macaísta, the language of the Macaense is a Portuguese creole with strong influences from what are now India and Malaysia as well as from China. Smaller numbers of words were introduced from the Philippines, Sri Lanka, Indonesia, Japan, and Britain while Portuguese words which died out in continental Portugal have been preserved in the dialect spoken by the Macaense. The Maquista dialect possesses three sub-dialects: 'pure Maquista', a modified Maquista which approaches standard Portuguese; and the Maquista which is spoken by Chinese. 'Pure Maquista' is spoken by the lower classes of Macaense whereas modified Maquista is used by the upper classes.

The Maquista dialect is under severe threat from standard Portuguese and, with the return of Macau to Chinese control in 1999, from Cantonese and standard Chinese as well, although attempts have been made to reverse this trend. In particular, José dos Santos Ferreira has devoted a tremendous amount of effort to the cause of the lingu Maquista, and although his efforts are unlikely to prove successful, they do at least mean that a considerable amount of Maquista literature and vocabulary has been recorded for posterity.

Today, some form of Portuguese language dominates in the home and school of the Macaense, although Cantonese is learned on the street and from the mother or father if they are Chinese. It is common for all mixed marriage children and for the Macaense in general to be fluent in spoken Cantonese but largely unable to read Chinese.

The Cantonese: Macau's majority

The overwhelming majority of Macau's population are Cantonese. Originating from the province of Guangdong in southern China which borders Macau, the Cantonese make up roughly eighty-five per cent of the territory's population.

Although Macau's majority, the Cantonese have a restricted

feeling of identity with the territory's heritage. The Cantonese generally view the current system of Portuguese administration, with its privileges for the Portuguese and the Macaense, as a burden of expedience. Since the majority left Guangdong for economic and political reasons, so long as their income is higher and their lifestyle less restricted than it was in Guangdong they will be willing to tolerate the discrepancies in housing, income and job opportunities. Older Cantonese have been quite satisfied with the growth in economic prosperity which they have experienced and so have remained content to leave administrative matters to the Portuguese and Macaense. However, this attitude is changing rapidly.

The term Cantonese also refers to a Chinese language, also known as Yuè, spoken in parts of Guangdong and Guangxi provinces. Within Macau there are several dialects of Cantonese, the most important of which is the Zhongshan dialect, named after Zhongshan Xian, the county bordering Macau. The Zhongshan dialect is further sub-divided into several sub-dialects. Of these the Shiqi sub-dialect was traditionally predominant in Macau. Today, however, standard Cantonese based on Guangzhou pronunciation dominates the speech of Macau.

When traditional Chinese ways are abandoned, the Chinese are opting for American, Japanese or Hong Kong-style Westernization rather than Portuguese or European customs. At the same time, in Macau and Hong Kong, one can find many traditional aspects of Chinese culture rarely seen on the mainland or on Taiwan.

The Cantonese culture of Macau, however, has little to distinguish it from that of Hong Kong. The language is the same although the Cantonese of Macau have incorporated fewer English words into their speech. The Chinese of Hong Kong often say that Macau's Chinese seem slower paced, although this is no doubt changing as Macau's economy picks up speed. Before the founding of Teledifusão de Macau in 1984, Macau's Chinese community watched Hong Kong television and the influence of Hong Kong is very obvious. This media dominance by Hong Kong has helped Macau's Chinese to assimilate some English-speaking culture whereas the cultural gap between them and the tiny Macaense and Portuguese communities remains rather large.

The Portuguese: Macau's administrators

The political and cultural rôle of Portugal in Macau is out of all proportion to the numbers of Portuguese residents in the territory. It is hard to say how many Portuguese there have been in Macau at any one time since statistics have often lumped other colonials and the Macaense into the Portuguese category, but, in general, the proportion of Chinese to Portuguese in Macau has increased over the centuries. In the 1560s, the Portuguese were about eight per cent of Macau's population. By the beginning of the 19th century, the Portuguese made up one third of the territory's people. During the 20th century, the number of Chinese has increased rapidly. In contrast, Portuguese numbers have risen only modestly with their proportion of the population remaining around two to three per cent since the 1920s.

Today, the majority of Portuguese in Macau are administrators often sent on contract for a fixed number of years. As such, they have little feeling of identity with Macau as home, much the same as most British in Hong Kong. Few Portuguese residents make the effort to learn Cantonese and often prefer using English to communicate with Macau's non-Portuguese-speaking community. Since the signing of the Sino-Portuguese accord over Macau in 1987, the small number who have committed themselves to making Macau their home are now likely to decrease while the numbers willing to remain after 1999 are also likely to be very small.

Portugal has had a policy of promoting Portuguese language, history and culture through publications and active support of 124 universities in different countries. In East Asia, Portugal has not had great success with these programmes and all hopes for an increased rôle for Portuguese culture in East Asia now hinge on Macau. The inclusion of Portuguese as an official language of Macau during the fifty year 'transition period' after 1999 is one positive achievement.

Apart from the Macaense, the Cantonese and the Portuguese, other ethnic groups, small in numbers but significant in impact, include the Fujianese, the Shanghainese, and the British.

The Fujianese

Historically, the rôle of the Fujianese (or Fukienese) in the formation of Macau was significant. Today, however, they represent a small minority of immigrants.

Recent Fujianese immigrants mostly speak various dialects of the Southern Mín language although there are some Northern Mín speakers as well. It has been estimated that there are around 30,000 Fujianese speakers in Macau. The original Fujian immigrants of the 16th century are now completely integrated into the Cantonese speaking majority.

The Shanghainese

The Shanghainese and their neighbours from the lower Chang Jiang delta speak various dialects of the Wú language and their presence in Macau is far more recent than that of the Fujianese or the Cantonese. Significant numbers of Shanghainese began to arrive in Macau during World War II and again during the subsequent civil war between the Communists and the Nationalists. While many more Shanghainese went to Hong Kong, some stayed in Macau because of connections with the Portuguese in Shanghai or because they could not get into Hong Kong.

It is estimated that there are around 30,000 speakers of Wú in Macau. As the younger generation are all taught Cantonese in schools, this community will probably be assimilated into the Cantonese majority within a generation, provided that significant numbers of Shanghainese do not arrive in the future.

The British and other Westerners

Other Westerners, beside the Portuguese, were involved in the development of Macau from a very early date and some even took part in Portugal's voyages of discovery. In the case of Macau, the privilege of the 'padroado do Oriente', whereby the Portuguese crown was given rights to establish all churches in the East, meant that Catholic priests of various nationalities were sent to Macau if they were to be involved in missionary work in China. In the early years of the settlement, Italian, Spanish, Flemish, and German priests all worked in Macau.

Since the 19th century, the British have played a strong rôle in the development of Macau, even using the territory as the headquarters for the British East India Company's China operations, prior to the founding of Hong Kong in 1841. The rise of Britain to naval dominance in the 19th century and the long alliance between Britain and Portugal combined with Chinese attempts to concentrate the activity of all Westerners in Macau all help to explain this phenomenon.

Since Macau is very dependent on Hong Kong and because English has become the dominant commercial and diplomatic language of East and Southeast Asia, the British continue to play a relatively important rôle, especially in Macau's education system. Until recently, most courses at the University of East Asia on Taipa were taught in English and the University has a British academic structure.

Religion

Traditional Chinese forms of worship

When the Portuguese arrived in Macau in the 16th century, the local Chinese were already practising traditional Chinese forms of worship similar to those found in other parts of south China. The worship of Mǎ Zǔ, the Goddess of the Sea, to whom the Má Kók

Introduction

Temple is dedicated, seems to have originated along the coast of Fujian province and to have come south with the early Fujianese settlers. Traditional Chinese religious practices have evolved and continued in Macau right up to the present day.

Although the large temples are now tourist spots, Macau's people still worship in them. Among the most famous are the Má Kók Temple, probably dating from the 13th century, the Kun Iam Temple, a complex of altars and gardens dedicated to the Goddess of Mercy, the Lin Fong Temple or Temple of the Lotus and the Tái Sôi Temple or Temple of the Year.

Catholicism

History   Wherever the Portuguese expanded their empire they brought Christianity with them. The Portuguese, Álvaro Margulhão, may have been the first Catholic priest to arrive on the south China coast in 1521. Soon after, many priests, not all of them Portuguese, began to arrive in the Macau area on board the annual Portuguese carrack from Goa or Malacca. The most famous of these priests was the Spaniard, Frances Xavier, who died at the Portuguese trading outpost on Shangchuan Island southwest of Macau in 1552.

Macau became the recognized centre of East Asian Christendom in 1576 when the Diocese of Macau was formally established with jurisdiction over China, Japan, Korea, and Cochin-China. After 1581, many Italian priests, first arriving in Macau, began to have more influence in Beijing than their Portuguese and Spanish colleagues. The most notable of these was Matteo Ricci. In 1588, the Diocese of Macau was slightly reduced in size and the Diocese of Funai (now the city of Oita, in Kyūshū) was created with jurisdiction for Japan.

Disagreement between various Catholic religious orders arose as early as the 17th century over political control of mission work and approaches to conversion of the Chinese to Christianity. The most contentious issue was the so-called 'rites controversy'. The Jesuits felt that ancestor worship and Confucian rites were not irreligious idolatry and held that the Chinese could become Catholic while still practising ancestor worship. Many Jesuits were even willing to adapt their own behaviour to fit in with Chinese customs. However, the Jesuits were opposed on the rites issue by the Dominicans and Franciscans. In 1715, Pope Clement XI condemned the practice of rites and missionaries were compelled to take an oath against them.

As a result of the controversy, Christians were banned in China from 1723. This caused difficulties for Chinese converts in Macau and, in 1759, the Jesuits were expelled from all Portuguese territories by Sebastião José de Carvalho e Melo, better known as the Marquês de Pombal. Effectively, Jesuits were expelled from Macau in 1762.

This expulsion was to be a serious set-back to the China missionary effort.

From 1784, the Lazarists were in control of the Seminary of São José and mission work continued until 1834, when all religious orders were repressed in Portugal. This repression affected Portuguese mission–based efforts in East Asia until the 1920s. The Communist takeover of mainland China, and the installation of their own version of the Catholic Church which does not recognize Papal authority, put an end to all missionary work in mainland China, concluding Macau's rôle in the China missions.

The Catholic church today   The Macaense are nearly 100 per cent Roman Catholic and have resisted intermixing Chinese religious practice with their Christian beliefs. The strong insistence on the part of the Catholic Church that its members do not engage in other religious worship is no doubt responsible for the strict separation.

Today, there are approximately 30,000 Catholics in Macau and the Diocese is composed of seven parishes: Sé Cathedral, which includes the town centre and reclaimed land along the Porto Exterior; São Lourenço, on the southwest of the peninsula; Santo António, along the Porto Interior; São Lázaro, landlocked in the centre of the peninsula and including Guia Hill; Nossa Senhora de Fátima, in the far north of Macau, created in the 20th century; Nossa Senhora do Carmo, on Taipa; and São Francisco Xavier, on Coloane.

In the city of Macau, churches began to proliferate in the late 16th and the first half of the 17th century. As fortresses were built, a chapel was constructed inside. In 1633–34 the Church of Nossa Senhora do Amparo was built and the founding of the Seminary of São José in 1728 meant that missionaries for China could be trained locally. However, by the 18th century, Macau was saturated with churches. It was not until 1885 that another church was built, this time on the Island of Taipa. In the 20th century, a few new churches have been constructed. In relation to Macau's population growth, however, expansion of the Catholic congregation has been small. Presumably the vast majority of recent Chinese immigrants have not shown a great interest in Christianity.

Feasts and processions   The most important religious feast specific to Macau is the feast and procession of St. John the Baptist on 24 June. The feast of Our Lady of Carmel is held in July at the Nossa Senhora do Carmo Church in Taipa. There is also a Lent procession which reenacts Christ's journey to his crucifixion.

British influence and the entry of Protestant sects

As Macau was the sole point of contact between all European

countries and China, it comes as no surprise that Protestant missions were eventually set up in Macau. In particular, the British East India Company was involved in the early Protestant mission activities

Surviving from the period of Protestant activity in Macau are two cemeteries and an Anglican Chapel, formerly the chapel of the British East India Company before they set up operation in Hong Kong. Services are still held in the Chapel on Sundays.

Other religions

An old Mohammedan mosque and the Parsee cemetery attest to the existence of other faiths in Macau's past. The Parsee cemetery bears the date 1829 on a plaque which indicates that this community thrived in Macau in connection with the British East India Company. One monument was erected as late as 1919.

Social conditions

Around the turn of the century, sanitation and living conditions for the majority of Macau's population were quite poor. The Chinese housing districts did not have sewerage systems and tuberculosis, veneral disease and other communicable diseases were rife, despite the efforts of the Santa Casa de Misericórdia and other charities.

Housing

Public housing in Macau dates back to 1928 when the first housing estate, Bairro Tamagnini Barbosa, was constructed in the northern part of the Macau peninsula. The influx of Chinese, following the fall of the Nationalists on the mainland, put Macau's housing under strain and, from this period, squatting was tolerated by the government. By the early 1970s, fourteen per cent of the total population on the Macau peninsula lived in squatter housing and ninety-nine per cent of the squatters were Chinese.

By the early 1970s, Macau was suffering a severe housing crisis, with an estimated shortage of 45,000 units. Rapid population growth in response to the economic boom in Macau at this time, coupled with the weak position of the Portuguese in the territory after 1966, meant that the government lacked the will or the funds to invest in public housing. In the early 1970s, public housing provided for only about five per cent of Macau's population and Macau has continued to lag behind Hong Kong in this area. However, the public housing in Macau, as in Hong Kong, has offered its residents better accommodation for their money than private sector housing.

In recent years, the government has tried to control the price of housing by contracts and, at the same time, to encourage the outright purchase of homes by enabling banks to provide credit to home buyers. There are plans for the upgrading of existing public housing in Taipa and on the peninsula.

Health

In 1985 and 1986 the government initiated a primary warning sub-system which has helped to improve health services in the territory. The Hospital Central Conde de São Januário remains the main government hospital with the Hospital Chinês Kiang Vu as Macau's other major hosptial. In 1987, renovation of the Hospital Central Conde de São Januário was the single major administrative investment item for the year. The government would like to construct two more hospitals to meet Macau's needs.

Security

Macau now maintains a Forças de Segurança or Security Force, since by agreement with China no Portuguese troops are to be stationed in the territory. The head of the Security Force is Portuguese but the staff are local people, largely Cantonese.

The economy

Macau has experienced rapid economic growth since the early 1970s. In particular, the export sector and tourist industries have expanded dramatically.

Between the years 1970 and 1979 the textile industry experienced a twenty-nine fold increase in total exports while the tourist industry benefitted from improved links with Hong Kong. In particular, exports to the European Economic Community (EEC) played an important part in stimulating the economy from 1970 to 1975 whereas links with the 'escudo block' (the Portuguese empire) began to waver. Although growth within Macau did not keep pace with export growth at this time, two major construction projects date from the early 1970s: the Hotel Lisboa, which was completed in 1970, and the Nobre de Carvalho Bridge, which linked Taipa to the peninsula in 1974.

The years 1975 to 1980 marked a transition period with Macau's political status altered to one of financial autonomy and an increase in investment from Hong Kong. Exports to the USA rose during the second half of the 1970s.

During the 1980s, the economy began to diversify away from textiles and casinos. There has been major growth in light industrial export items such as artificial flowers, toys, and, more recently, electronic and leather goods. Exports of these goods are now growing faster than textile exports. In general, however, the pace of growth has slowed down in the 1980s while more concern has been directed towards social welfare, improvement of the service sector, and administrative reform. Moreover, Macau's entrepreneurs have begun to invest in China and other markets overseas to a much greater degree than in the past.

The market for Macau's exports has also changed significantly since 1970. In that year, Portuguese Africa, West Germany, Hong Kong, France and Portugal were major markets. By 1986, however, the USA, Hong Kong, France and West Germany remained important partners while Portugal, Africa, Latin America and the Soviet block were insignificant markets and exports to the UK and the People's Republic of China had increased significantly. In particular, exports to the USA have been growing in recent years.

Imports can be difficult to measure as much passes through Hong Kong. In addition to Hong Kong, the People's Republic of China, Japan, the USA and the EEC are the major sources of imports. Hong Kong and the People's Republic of China together accounted for more than sixty per cent of Macau's imports in 1987.

Another recent trend is the increased linking of Macau's economy to the Zhuhai special economic zone to the north of the peninsula in the People's Republic of China. Already some Macau (and Hong Kong) industrialists have set up branch plants in Zhuhai which are in some ways complementary to those they have in Macau. Capital from Macau has been invested in tourist projects in Zhuhai and a joint land reclamation project is planned. It remains to be seen whether Zhuhai will provide competition for Macau's economy or will complement it and aid in Macau's penetration of the Guangdong hinterland.

Simultaneously, the Chinese are beginning to invest in Macau in order to take advantage of the territory's infrastructure and also to prop up its economy should it begin to waver before 1999. Much of this investment is through the Nam Kwong Trading Company, established in 1949. In 1986, Nam Kwong was split into a political arm and a commercial trading company. Since that time, Nam Kwong has been exploring possibilities of joint ventures with foreign firms in Macau, and even invested, in 1988, in a trading company established to deal with Macau-Soviet trade.

Another major pro-China economic power in Macau is the Chinese Chamber of Commerce which was established in 1911. With almost three thousand members, the Chamber is closely involved in encouraging investment by Macau in Guangdong and promoting Macau's interests in China.

Agricultural products such as fresh water fish and, since 1984, electricity continue to be supplied by China for the local economy.

Finance and banking

Currency   Macau has its own currency, the pataca, which is divided into 100 avos. The term pataca seems to come from the Arabic word for window, bataca, and refers to a design on the back of a Spanish coin during the reign of Carlos IV (1788-1808) which had looked like a Moorish window. In East Asia, the Mexican dollar or pieces of eight was known in Portuguese as the Pataca Mexicana and reached the territory via the Philippines. Pataca was the name of former currencies in Brazil and Timor. Avo is a term used to indicate a fraction and was used as a currency term in Timor. However, these terms are only used in Macau nowadays. Macau was the only overseas Portuguese province never to adopt escudo as a currency name.

Pataca notes first appeared in Macau in 1906 and were issued by the Banco Nacional Ultramarino. Since 1980, the Instituto Emissor de Macau has been responsible for currency issue although the Banco Nacional Ultramarino remains the government's banker. This was the bank responsible for issuing new currency when coinage began in 1952. Prior to World War I, the effective currency in Macau was the silver tael, although many European currencies were also used in commerce. The Hong Kong dollar then came to dominate and now shares a leading position in Macau with the pataca.

In 1977, the pataca was freed from the escudo and pegged to the Hong Kong dollar. In February 1989, the pataca was untied from the Hong Kong dollar and can now be exchanged directly for Renminbi purchases in China. Both the pataca and the Hong Kong dollar circulate freely in the territory. The official pegged rate was fixed at Macau $1.03 to HK$1.00 and since February 1989 the Hong Kong dollar has remained stronger than the pataca. As a consequence, everyone is willing to accept Hong Kong dollars on even exchange. For large purchases one can get Hong Kong dollars changed into patacas at the formal rate.

Banking   A banking ordinance passed in 1982 allowed for the establishment of development banks. As a result, Macau gained a development bank, Sociedade Financeira, and a Macau bank association, Associação de Bancos de Macau. In 1983 alone thirteen new banks were started which brought the total number in Macau to twenty-three, including nine local banks. In particular, Portuguese bankers see a future for Macau as an off-shore banking centre. In 1987, legislation was introduced which allowed foreign banks to operate tax-free after paying an annual fee.

China's banking interests in Macau are looked after by the Nám T'óng Bank, one of the Bank of China's thirteen Hong Kong-Macau banks. Nám T'óng was acquired by the Bank of China in 1987. It handles roughly thirty per cent of Macau's total bank deposits and has been heavily involved in loans to Zhuhai. This is one sign of China's growing financial presence in the territory.

Macau as entrepôt

During the 19th century, Macau was still involved in the re-export of Chinese tea and silk. However, in 1870, the Portuguese enforced tariffs to protect their own colonial products and shipping. Since none of the tea and silk was produced in Macau, these products fell out of the hands of Macau and the Portuguese. The opium re-export trade also declined when the Macau government began to monopolize the trade in 1927.

Today, official statistics indicate that the flow of Chinese goods through Macau for re-export is insignificant. In the period 1983-85, however, a significant illegal re-export trade in Chinese antiques was passing through the city. This trade, while it lasted, perhaps reached totals of £110 million.

Re-export of non-Chinese imports from Macau to China grew in 1984-85 but slowed in 1986. This slow-down, caused by Chinese import restrictions, could well be temporary, especially as Macau will shortly be linked by dual carriage motorway to Guangzhou while a railway will link Zhuhai and Guangzhou. These links, combined with the improved port at Ká Hó on Coloane, could lead to Macau becoming the entrepôt for the west side of the Pearl River delta.

Industry

Although recent industrial growth in Macau has been rapid, the major reasons for this growth have been the availability of cheap labour coupled with laissez-faire government. Industrial production stagnated in the late 1970s, but, from 1983, it has been rising rapidly. Much of the industrial growth is due to investors from Hong Kong taking advantage of the cheap unskilled labour and lower land prices, and being able to export goods under a Macau rather than a Hong Kong quota to certain countries with protectionist tendencies. Productivity in Macau remains lower than in Hong Kong although the gap is narrowing rapidly and compares favourably with pro-ductivity in the People's Republic of China. Light industry has always been and continues to be more important than heavy industry in Macau's economy. Shortages of water and electricity dictate that the government will promote high technology industries.

The textile industry showed some growth prior to the 1974 revolution in Portugal with trade between Macau and Portuguese Africa as well as with Portugal itself. In the 1970s, textiles led Macau's rapid economic growth. Today textile and garment exports are still a major factor in Macau's economy and accounted for roughly three-quarters of the value of all exports in 1986. This concentration on textiles is a matter of concern to some members of the Macau government who will no doubt try to encourage diversification away from this sector. Growth in textiles will be hampered anyway as Macau has reached its quota limitations for imports to the USA and the EEC.

During the early 1980s, light industry in Macau diversified into the manufacture of toys, artificial flowers, leather articles and electronic goods. Together, these items amounted to about twenty per cent of the total export figures for 1986. The USA and the EEC received large shares of these exports.

Agriculture and fishing

Early maps show only minimal agricultural activity within the wall on the Macau peninsula. Today, what agriculture there remains is restricted to market gardening in the Antigo Hipódomo in the extreme northeast and pockets on the lowlands of Taipa and the small valleys of Coloane. Market gardening in Macau is under threat from land redevelopment to an even greater degree than in Hong Kong.

Fishing has always been an important activity in Macau and was the mainstay of Macau's primary production, along with limited rice farming on Coloane, in the early part of the 20th century.

Tourism and diversions

Tourism has grown rapidly during the 1980s with a marked increase in hotels and other facilities. In addition to the traditional day gamblers from Hong Kong, a more heterogeneous tourist population is now visiting the peninsula and islands.

In 1988, there were 5.54 million tourist arrivals by sea representing an 8.68 per cent increase over 1987. Jetfoils from Hong Kong bring in the largest proportion of tourists followed by high speed ferries and hydrofoils with the older ferryboats carrying an increasingly smaller proportion of tourists. Despite changes in tourist habits, gambling remains Macau's most popular tourist diversion and Hong Kong the most important source of visitors. In order to cater to this group an all night jetfoil service to Hong Kong was introduced in July 1989. Hong Kong residents make up four-fifths of the tourist arrivals in

Introduction

Macau with the greatest influx of gamblers at weekends. The major nationalities of foreign visitors to Macau are, in order of importance, Japanese, American, British, Taiwan Chinese, Thai and Australian. The recent lifting of travel restrictions on Taiwan has meant a considerable increase in the number of Republic of China nationals entering Macau on their way to visit the People's Republic. In addition, more South Koreans are visiting the People's Republic of China via Macau.

Hotel construction

From 1982 to 1986, five new hotels opened in Macau bringing the total number to twenty-two. In 1983, there were only two de-luxe hotels in Macau but by 1986 there were four five star hotels. The number of guest houses and pousadas has remained more or less the same throughout the 1980s. At the end of 1988, there were 3,395 hotel rooms, forty-five rooms in inns and 1,085 rooms in guest houses.

As much of Macau's hotel business comes from weekend visitors to the casinos, hotel occupancy rates have been low during the week (sixty per cent in 1985). This loading problem leads to discounts for weekday visitors and difficulties in booking a room at weekends. It also means that further construction of hotels will only be undertaken with some caution, although three new hotels are scheduled for 1989.

Gambling

Gambling has been popular in China for centuries and the Chinese were probably gambling in Macau from a very early date. It has never been considered a crime in Macau and the majority of citizens view the activity as a part of life.

Licensed gambling was introduced in Macau by the Governor Isidoro Francisco Guimarães (1851-63) in order to secure revenue for the new province which had been separated from Goa in 1844. The licensing was a success from the start.

After 1934, when the Tai Hing Company obtained monopoly rights, gambling became highly organized. Under Tai Hing's leaders, what is now the Hotel Central in the town's centre became the home of Macau's major casinos. Other casinos were located on the Rua da Felicidade and the Rua 5 de Outubro. The major games at this period were all Chinese: fantan, p'ai kao, and dai sui.

Macau's gambling industry was given a major boost when the Communists came to power in 1949 and banned gambling in the People's Republic of China. Guangzhou had long been a major gambling centre but from 1949 it was no longer in competition with Macau.

The rôle of gambling in Macau's economy was further entrenched in 1962 when the casino games were taken over by a new syndicate, the Sociedade de Turismo e Diversões de Macau (STDM or Macau Travel and Amusement Company) under the leadership of Stanley Ho. Whereas the Tai Hing Company had been paying Macau $300,000 a year in taxes, the STDM bought the gambling rights for three million patacas a year. In 1977, the base payment of the STDM was raised to Macau $30 million a year. Since 1982, the payment has been on a percentage basis with the initial twenty-five per cent to be increased annually by one per cent from 1986 to reach a new level of thirty per cent by 1991. The STDM rights also include the operation of the ferry services between Hong Kong and Macau which they have greatly improved. In total, the STDM employs 10,000 people in a wide range of occupations.

The STDM introduced Western-style gambling games to Macau and now the big money is derived from these games rather than from traditional Eastern-style diversions. Gambling accounts for roughly twenty per cent of Macau's gross domestic product and it is said that the STDM contribution to the budget may be up to thirty per cent of the total. Macau today is the gambling centre of East Asia and it is likely to remain so for a considerable period after the reversion of Macau to Chinese administration in 1999. It is said that China will be willing to extend the STDM franchise for another twenty years after it expires in 1992. At the same time, the Chinese are thinking of taking a lesson from Macau and allowing gambling in their newly created Hainan province.

Casinos   Casino gambling is the basis of much of Macau's tourism with roughly four million players a year and as such it is the mainstay of the territory's economy. The majority of casino customers have always been Chinese. Up until 1949 most came from China but since that date the people of Hong Kong have dominated the casinos.

Under the STDM, casino operations began in 1963 in the Hotel Estoril and on a converted junk, the predecessor of the present Macau Palace, which was famous for the use of baskets to allow betting on the upper floor. Today, there are six casinos in the city listed here in order of popularity: the Casino Lisboa (opened in 1970) in the Hotel Lisboa; the Casino Oriental (opened in 1984); the Casino Macau Palace (on a boat anchored in the Porto Interior); the Casino Jai Alai (opened in 1975) in the jai alai fronton; the Casino Kâm Pêk (opened in 1963 and renovated in 1988) and the new casino in the Hyatt Regency Macau (opened in 1988). The casinos are open twenty-four hours a day with about three million patacas' worth of chips bet per hour for a total of around twenty-five billion patacas bet per annum.

Introduction

Western-style casino games found in Macau include baccarat (the most popular game), blackjack, roulette, boule, slot machines (a total of 625 in the city) and craps. Eastern-style games include p'ai kao (Chinese dominoes formerly played in homes and restaurants), fantan, and dai siu (also called cussec, a dice game). Today, blackjack as played in Macau has its own rules, the most infamous being that the biggest better, not the person holding the cards, decides upon how a hand is played.

Dog racing Another form of gambling for which Macau is famous is dog racing. Dog racing did not begin in Macau until 1963. Its founding father was a British entrepreneur who had years of experience in the Shanghai tracks. The greyhounds came mainly from Australia but recently some have been imported from Britain. From its inception, the sport attracted mainly Hong Kong people and the track (or canidrome) was only registered in Macau when the government insisted upon local registration. In 1984, Fly Gain Limited, a subsidiary of STDM, gained control of sixty per cent of the stock in the canidrome. The track is rented from the government for a fixed rent of Macau $200,000 per annum. Races are held three nights a week and attendance has always been good. In terms of relative importance, dog racing is the second most lucrative form of gambling, albeit by a good distance, after the casinos.

Jai alai Not far from the pier on the Porto Exterior is the Palácio Jai Alai or jai alai fronton, a modern structure encompassing 34,000 square metres built in 1974, where the sport jai alai is played and, in true Macau tradition, gambled over. The game, also known as pelota basca, is said to have been brought to Macau before World War II from Manila where it was introduced by the Spanish. The current concession for jai alai, however, dates from 1971 and games began in 1972. Most of the leading jai alai players are Basques, although Macau also produces some players. The game is played with a racket (cesta) and ball (pelota) which is said to move at a speed of 150 miles per hour, so giving jai-alai its reputation as the world's fastest game.

Harness racing There was horse racing in Macau as early as 1829, but the old race track, the Hipódromo, located in the northeast portion of the Macau peninsula, is now a squatter settlement area. In 1977, an agreement was signed to establish a harness race track on Taipa and the concession known as the Companhia de Corridas de Cavalos a Trote com Atrelade finished construction of the track in 1980. The majority of spectators came from Hong Kong whereas the largest group of jockeys came from Australia. Capital outlay for construction of the track proved very expensive and local interest has not been sufficient to consider the operation a success. Part of the problem has been that horse racing is legal in Hong Kong. In 1988, the Companhia ceased on-course operations and, in 1989, a newly formed Macau Jockey Club took over the race track.

Instantaneous lotteries   Lottery tickets went on sale on 16 December 1984 with the intention that funds should be used by the Fundaçao Macau or Macau Foundation for 'cultural, beneficiary, and educational' ends. In 1985, sales of instantaneous lottery tickets amounted to eighteen million patacas, leaving a gross of around ten million patacas. The most important of these lotteries, pák ká piu, has three draws a day and betting centres throughout the city.

'Sin city'

Macau has often been portrayed as a city of sin where all vices could be satisfied. A Franciscan friar visiting the territory between 1742 and 1745 described Macau as being dominated by 'lechery, robbery, treachery, gambling, drunkenness and other vices'. Right up until the 20th century gambling, drugs, gold smuggling, and prostitution were somewhat interlinked, with further connections to the triads. Although none of these activities has disappeared in Macau, they are all, with the exception of gambling, in decline, leaving Macau with only a whiff of its early atmosphere of sin.

Drugs

In 1935, it was stated that Macau had twenty-seven licensed retail opium shops and sixty-nine smoking dens. The government opium monopoly supplied twenty per cent of the territory's revenue. Before 1951, opium was being processed into heroin in Macau and sold on the Rua da Felicidade but this centre was closed following a visit to Macau by a United Nations commission. Reports indicate that opium was still smuggled from China to Macau during the 1960s and that heroin could still be purchased discreetly. Marijuana was never popular in Macau. A drug clinic has been set up on Taipa for first offence users.

Gold smuggling

Gold smuggling became big business in post-World War II Macau because Portugal did not sign the Bretton Woods agreement of 1946 which prohibited signatories from importing gold for private use. Soon gold smuggling in Macau was monopolized and handled by the Ng Fuk Tong or Five Good Fortunes Association, a branch of the gambling monopoly, the Tai Hing Company. The man who represented the Macau government in the signing of the gold monopoly agreements, Pedro José Lobo, was also involved in the gold smuggling and died in 1956, a very wealthy man.

Since the importing of gold was entirely legal, government figures were issued showing that between sixteen and twenty million ounces of gold were brought into Macau annually between 1949 and 1966. Not suprisingly, the government did not produce gold export figures. It is said that once gold arrived in Macau it was melted into bars and then smuggled via Hong Kong to countries where people were willing to pay a high price for gold since they mistrusted the local currency. It has been stated that Macau's gold was important to China. In reality, the majority seems to have gone to other Asian countries such as India. China, however, may have been involved in some of the gold trade through its Macau banks.

Prostitution

Prostitution is not a new business in Macau. Legislation on prostitution did not begin until 1900 when provisions were laid down for the registering of prostitutes. Even though Portugal signed an International Convention in May 1910 requiring it to legislate against prostitution, no laws were enacted in Macau at that time. In 1925, however, the Macau police adopted a set of severe anti-prostitution laws. In particular, these laws made it illegal for minors under sixteen years of age to frequent licensed houses. Those who let such minors into houses were to be punished by a prison sentence of not more than six months. There were other laws against inducing people to become prostitutes. However, the police were known not to enforce these laws and could easily be bribed. There is even a report from the 1920s of a house which 'specialized' in twelve to fourteen year-old girls.

Once a woman was licensed she was prohibited from living near churches, schools and public parks, a virtual impossibility in Macau. As a consequence, this regulation was commonly broken. Licensed women could not move house without first informing the police. Women with venereal disease were not allowed to continue their work but, as there was no relief for them, probably very few stopped working.

By 1960, there were an estimated one thousand prostitutes in Macau, but already it was becoming hard to bribe the police and business was more difficult than in the early 1950s. The traditional centre for prostitution was the auspiciously named Rua da Felicidade or Happiness Street while, in the 1950s and 1960s, the soldiers from Mozambique and Angola had their own down-market district on the Beco da Rosa or Rose Lane.

In recent years, with the troops gone and the local economy prosperous, the business has been 'modernized' with massage parlours gaining in popularity. The majority of massage parlour hostesses are from Thailand.

Triads

Triads, known in Cantonese as Sam Hôp Wui and in Standard Chinese as Sān Hé Hùi, are the Chinese equivalent of the mafia. These organizations are criminal brotherhoods which operate various vices as well as legal operations. In the past, the government has relied on competition between groups and, since 1934, on the first gambling syndicate, the Tai Hing Company, to control the triads.

The triads are still present in Macau and it is said that even the new gambling monopoly established in 1962, the STDM, pays off the triads to preserve order although it appears that no member of the STDM management belongs to the triads. Other major organizations in Macau, including the Chinese business organizations, probably have some sort of 'relationship' worked out with the triads. The government appears to be in no position to control triad activities and there have even been accusations that government casino inspectors belong to these organizations. Today, the triads are said to run loan shark operations near the casinos as their main source of funds. Triads are also involved in prostitution operations, forcing Hong Kong girls to work off debts with up to forty per cent interest per week.

Transportation

Shipping

Ships have always been important to Macau. In the 1950s, three daily passenger journeys between Hong Kong and Macau were undertaken by large ships with a carrying capacity of 6,144. In 1964, the number of daily vessel journeys was increased to four and, in the same year, hydrofoils were introduced with five runs a day. In 1965, the hydrofoil runs were doubled to ten and total daily passenger capacity increased to 10,532. By the 1980s, vessels were travelling between Macau and Guangzhou as well as Jiangmen. Following the lifting of Nationalist Chinese travel restrictions to Macau and to mainland China in 1988, a twice-weekly ferry service between Macau and Taiwan was introduced. Only one of the older ferry boats now remains in service and this is likely to be withdrawn shortly.

The majority of Macau's shipping is floated over on barges from Hong Kong. However, attempts to create a direct container service are already under way. Possibilities for a substantial freight service hinge on developments at the new Ká Hó port on Coloane.

Roads

Plans have been put forward to build a high-speed motorway linking Zhuhai to Guangzhou and Guangzhou to Shenzhen on the Hong Kong border. The road linking Macau to Zhongshan (Shiqi) and Guangzhou was only built in 1928.

Locally, there is a plan to build a tunnel through Guia Hill connecting with a second bridge across to Taipa. New road building is continuing in recently urbanized areas. In addition to this, the government has become worried about the mixture of pedestrians and automated traffic in congested parts of the city and is building pedestrian bridges in an attempt to relieve the congestion caused by the rapid increase in the number of vehicles.

Airport

Several schemes for an airport in Macau have been proposed during the 1980s. In 1983, a feasibility study was completed and a revised version of this study remains the basis for construction plans. It appears that an airport will be built on reclaimed land to the east of Taipa and Coloane. The airport is scheduled for completion in 1993 and should be able to handle jumbo-jets. Zhuhai had also intended to build an airport, but is now planning to cooperate in the construction of the Macau airport. Both the Portuguese and the Chinese civil aviation authorities are participating in the consortium set up to build the airport and no doubt theirs will be the airlines to use the Macau airport.

Helicopters are due to begin scheduled flights to Hong Kong from a helipad adjacent to the Porto Exterior in 1989. The helicopters are to be serviced on Coloane.

Railways

In 1877, there was a proposal to build a railway from Macau to Guangzhou. An accord signed in Shanghai in 1904 to build the line alarmed Hong Kong but construction never began, presumably because of the Portuguese and Chinese revolutions of 1910 and 1911. In 1988, the Guangdong authorities announced that they hoped to complete a 100 kilometre rail line linking Zhuhai to Guangzhou by 1990. Although unlikely to cross the border into Macau, this rail link with have a great impact on the territory.

Communications

Telecommunications

Macau was slow to develop modern telecommunications and the territory's network is currently being modernized. The establishment of a satellite ground station on Coloane, in 1984, allowed direct communications with Portugal, Japan, and the UK. Between the years 1982 and 1986 the number of telephone lines tripled while the number of international direct dialing destinations increased from one to 121. Telex use has also been increasing in recent years. Over half the telex origins and destinations are Hong Kong with Portugal as the second most important place of origin and destination. In 1986, plans were announced to install a fifteen kilometre optic fibre cable between Macau and Zhuhai which would improve co-ordination between the economies of the two territories.

Television and radio

Teledifusão de Macau (TDM) television began broadcasting on 13 May 1984. The Macau government had made an agreement for the television station to receive technical assistance from Portugal's national television network (RTP) and hired local people to broadcast. At present, TDM television runs both Portuguese and Cantonese programmes on the same channel but there are moves to create separate Cantonese and Portuguese channels along the lines of the Hong Kong networks.

Even now, Hong Kong stations are watched in Macau. TDM television cannot be received on many Hong Kong television sets although TDM plans to build a five kilowatt transmission centre on Coloane. Retransmission at higher power could begin soon which would enable sixty to seventy per cent of Hong Kong's people to watch Macau television. It is expected that the new separate Cantonese channel proposed by the Macau government, which may be a private concession, would then begin to have some impact in Hong Kong.

TDM operates two radio stations, one broadcasting in Portuguese and the other in Cantonese. In addition there is one private station operating in Cantonese, Emissora Vila Verde.

Utilities

The government made significant outlays to develop public utilities in the early 1980s. Capital for these improvements in water and electricity came mainly from the 1983 contract with the STDM

Introduction

gambling syndicate. Since 1984, Macau's electricity supply has been linked to the Guangdong power grid with the proportion of electricity supplied from China likely to increase greatly in the coming years. Water supplies are critical, especially to the development of the islands, but Macau's supply should increase when a new reservoir is completed thirteen kilometres away in Guangdong. However, there will still be problems getting this water to Taipa and Coloane.

Education

Macau has played a key rôle in the transmission of Western knowledge, particularly science and philosophy, to the East and in the acquisition of Eastern knowledge, particularly philosophy, by the West. In 1597, the first Western degree courses in East Asia were organized at the Madre De Deus School next to the Jesuits' residence on Macau. Courses in theology, Greek and Latin, rhetoric and philosophy were introduced at this time and, by 1601, there were language, music and painting schools as well.

In 1728, the Jesuits opened the Seminary of São José where educational activities continued until 1762 when the Jesuits were expelled from Macau. This began a period of educational decline which was only reversed with the return of the Jesuits in 1862. Another important event occurred in 1878 when the Association for the Promotion of the Instruction of the Macaense opened a business school. This school operated in cooperation with the Seminary of São José from 1881 to 1910.

In 1882 and 1884, education began on the islands when three schools for Chinese boys were established on Taipa, Coloane, and Xiaohengqin. The government continued to build schools on the disputed islands with Chinese schools built on Xiaohengqin in 1917 and on Dahengqin in 1927. On the peninsula, a Liceu Central was opened in 1894 and a Central Primary School in 1894. Other state schools followed, including the Luso-Chinese Primary School in 1919 and the Escola Infantil in 1923.

Private Chinese schools operated in Macau from at least as early as 1800. Several private schools were established in the late 19th and early 20th centuries.

Modern primary and secondary education in Macau operates in three language-modes, Luso-Chinese, English-Chinese, and Portuguese. Teaching in Portuguese is largely for continental Portuguese residents in Macau whereas the other two language-groupings are more widely used by the Chinese population. Higher education is limited to the Universidade da Ásia Oriental, or University of East Asia, on Taipa, where the teaching is largely in English.

1

The arts

In 1982, the government formed the Instituto Cultural de Macau to promote Luso-Chinese cultural interchange. Generous funding has allowed many publications concerning Macau to appear under its sponsorship in recent years. The Institute also sponsors cultural displays and events.

Macau has several fine museums. The Museu Luís de Camões is most famous for its collection of Western-style China trade paintings, the Sun Yat-sen Memorial House commemorates the Chinese republican leader who practised medicine in Macau and the Museu e Centro de Estudos Marítimos de Macau (Museum and Centre of Maritime Studies) has recently opened. There is also a Correois e Telecomincações (Postage and Telecommunications) Museum located in the Central Post Office building.

Libraries include the Biblioteca do Complexo Escolar de Macau, the Biblioteca Nacional de Macau, the Arquivo Histórico de Macau, and the library of the University of East Asia. The Arquivo Histórico de Macau contains documents recording the history of Macau from its origins up to about fifty years ago. Many of the rarest documents have been put on microfilm and there is a photograph collection.

Literature

Much of the writing done by Macaense authors has spread beyond the territory and made its imprint on Portuguese language communities throughout East Asia. The Macaense have founded newspapers in Guangzhou, Shanghai, Kōbe, and Hong Kong.

Some of Macau's most famous writers include the poet, Leonel Alves, Deolinda da Conceição, author of *A Cabaia*, a collection of short stories, and Henrique de Senna Fernandes, author of *Nám Ván* and *Amor e Dedinhos de Pé*. The Portuguese author, Camilo de Almeida Pessanha lived in Macau for thirty-two years, died in the city during 1926 and is buried there. His most famous works are *Clépsidra* (1920), and *Clépsidra e Outros Poemas* (1926). José de Santos Ferreira is the most famous living literary figure writing in the Maquista dialect of Portuguese. He is well known for his poems and short stories.

Art

During the 17th and 18th centuries, Macau was regularly depicted in Chinese woodblock prints and European prints. Some of these European-based landscape views show the impact of the Chinese water-colour tradition in the use of a hand scroll format, as well as in some aspects of style and technique. From the mid-19th century onwards, these China trade paintings became extremely commercialized as export items for Europe. Towards the end of the 19th century, some of the detail of Macau begins to show inaccuracies. This is no doubt due to the fact that many of these paintings were done in Guangzhou, Hong Kong or other treaty ports and not in Macau.

During the 18th century, views of Macau usually featured the Praia Grande, the Porto Interior or aerial views of the city. In the 19th century, artists began to explore more varied aspects of Macau such as the city's churches, temples, buildings and people.

George Chinnery (1774-1852) is the most famous painter of Macau. After working for many years in Dublin, London, and India, he arrived in the territory in 1825 and stayed for twenty-seven years. Chinnery came to East Asia in order to flee his creditors in South Asia and Macau must have appealed to this rather vain, profligate painter because of the large English-speaking population outside the British law. Friendship with the wealthy merchant, William Jardine, in India facilitated his establishment in Macau and he made his living by painting portraits of wealthy Europeans and Chinese in Guangzhou, in Macau, and, after 1841, in Hong Kong. Chinnery left behind numerous sketches of the life of the common Chinese as well as scenes of Macau and, with their strongly European flavour, his paintings provide a significant contrast to the established Chinese genre.

Also active in Macau during the 19th century was the French artist, Auguste Borget (1808-77). Borget and Chinnery exchanged paintings and the Frenchman went on to rival the Irishman at portraying the life of the common people in Macau, Guangzhou and Hong Kong. While travelling around the world Borget spent six months in Macau and four months visiting points along the Guangdong and Fujian coasts. Some of Borget's sketches were published in his book *La Chine et Les Chinois*, which appeared in Paris in 1842. Copies of Borget's lithographs were reproduced, without acknowledgement, in *China Illustrated* during the 1840s and 1850s and it was these copies that came to represent Macau in the minds of many around the world.

Other famous painters of Macau include Cheong Chiu Ch'ün, Luís Demée, Herculano Estorninho, Lâm Kân, and Yü Kwân Wâi whose pen name is Hâng Sâm.

Macau and 1999

After 1999, the chief executive or Governor of Macau will be appointed by the Chinese government. The 'special administrative region of Macau, China' is intended to have a legislature with a majority of elected members and all inhabitants of Macau will become citizens of the Republic of China. Those with Portuguese passports will be allowed to retain them for travel purposes, although the Chinese are not in favour of dual citizenship.

Like Hong Kong, the special administrative region of Macau is to have a fifty year period during which the capitalist system and the territory's autonomy are supposed to be maintained. During this period, Portuguese will remain an official language and it is hoped by the Portuguese that Macau will continue to be the focal point for Portuguese culture in East Asia.

The need to bolster the Portuguese presence in East Asia may have been a factor in Lisbon's granting of additional Portuguese passport rights. Up to 200,000 Macau Chinese will be allowed to apply for regular Portuguese passports by 1999, a decision which has annoyed both Beijing and London. The Chinese authorities regard the Chinese ethnic community of Macau as Chinese nationals and it will prove embarrassing and make Macau more difficult to administer should the majority of those eligible opt for Portuguese citizenship. For London, the Lisbon decision has been an embarrassment as the British government is not allowing similar rights of abode to the Hong Kong born holders of British National Overseas passports. In the light of the suppression of the Democracy movement during June 1989 which led to a demonstration of an estimated 100 thousand people in Macau (approximately one-fifth of the population), there now seems little doubt that most eligible ethnic Chinese will opt for Portuguese passports in the near future.

Citizenship and language commitments by Portugal assure that after 1999 Macau will continue to maintain that 'little difference' the territory has always had from Hong Kong. Nonetheless, the return of administration to the People's Republic of China will have the greatest impact on Macau of any event since the arrival of the Portuguese on the peninsula in the mid-16th century.

Glossary of Place Names

(E) – English, (P) – Portuguese, (Y) – Cantonese or Yuè, (M) – Standard Chinese or Mandarin

Name in text		Other names	
(M)	Baishaling	(P)	Passaleão
(M)	Beijing	(E)	Peking, (P) Pequim
(M)	Dahengqin	(P)	Montanha, (Y) Tai-Vong-Cam
(M)	Fujian	(E)	Fukien
(M)	Gansu	(E)	Kansu
(M)	Guangdong	(E)	Canton province, Kwangtung
(M)	Guangzhou	(E)	Canton, Kwangchow
(P)	Ilha Verde	(E)	Green Island, (Y) Ch'êngchâu, (M) Qingzhōu
(P)	Macau	(E,P)	Macao, (Y) Ou Mun, (M) Aòmén
(M)	Neilingding	(E)	Lintin
(M)	Ningbo	(E)	Ningpo
(E)	Pearl River	(M)	Zhū Jiāng
(P)	Porta(s) do Cerco	(E)	Barrier Gate, (Y) Kwân cháp, (M) Guānzhá
(P)	Porto Exterior	(E)	Outer Harbour, (Y) Ngóikóng, (M) Wàigǎng
(P)	Porto Interior	(E)	Inner Harbour, (Y) Nóikóng, (M) Nèigǎng
(P)	Praia Grande	(Y)	Nám Van, (M) Nán Wān
(M)	Quanzhou	(E)	Ch'üanchou, Zayton
(M)	Tianjin	(E)	Tientsin
(M)	Wanzhai	(E)	Lapa Island, (P) Ilha da Lapa
(M)	Xiaohengqin	(P)	Dom João, Macarira, (Y) Sio-Vong-Cam
(M)	Zhejiang	(E)	Chekiang
(M)	Zhenhai	(E)	Chenhai

The Territory and Its People

1 **Macau: a short handbook.**
José Maria Braga.   Macau: Information and Tourism Department, 1970.
63p. map. bibliog.
In its day, this was a very good compendium of basic information about all aspects of
Macau. Today, however, it is only useful for its treatment of the political, economic,
and social situation of Macau in the 1960s. This book was often given away free by the
Information and Tourism Department and had editions in 1963, 1965, and 1968. In the
back is a list of Macau's Governors from 1623 to date.

2 **Viva Macau!**
Mark Brazier, Shann Davies.   Hong Kong: Macmillan, 1980. 131p.
Essentially a 'coffee table' book, this work presents many interesting facts about day-
to-day life in Macau although some of the historical information is more open to
question than the text implies. Despite the title the book is in English.

3 **Imagens de Macau.** (Images of Macau.)
Raquel Soeiro de Brito.   Lisbon: Agencia Geral do Ultramar, 1962. 52p.
9 maps.
Gives a general overview of Macau as it was in the early 1960s. The historical
geography of the city, presented in the first section, is followed by sections on
agriculture, boat life, Coloane and Taipa. This book contains one of the first known
land use maps of the Macau peninsula (Fig. 5, p. 19).

4 **Macau: city of commerce and culture.**
Edited by Rolf Dieter Cremer.   Hong Kong: UEA Press, 1987. 198p.
5 maps. bibliog.
This volume brings together essays on various aspects of Macau written by specialists.
Topics covered include origins and early history, history in world trade, the church,
paintings of Macau, geography, architecture, Chinese dialects, Portuguese language,

1

The Territory and Its People

cultural contact, the economy, gambling, the regional rôle of Macau, and the legal system. Some of these essays are listed as separate entries in this bibliography. One oddity of this book is that most proper names are romanized in Standard Chinese pinyin rather than in their common Macau Cantonese romanized form. Characters are provided which may help some readers but the different romanizations may confuse others.

5 Macau

Shann Davies   Singapore: Times Editions, 1986. 128p.

This book can be considered an updated, less expensive 'coffee table' book than *Viva Macau!* (q.v.). The photographs, by Leong Ka Tai, and text give a good flavour of all aspects of Macau in the mid-1980s. Tourist information is provided in the final section. Despite the fact that the text was written prior to the signing of the Sino-Portuguese joint declaration on Macau's future in 1987, the book is still quite up-to-date.

6 The Europa year book: a world survey.

Europa Publications.   London: The Author, 1926-, 2nd series, vol. 2. annual.

A four-page survey of Macau is included which gives more coverage of history, geography, and general statistics than does the *Asia yearbook* (q.v.). As a consequence, there is relatively little information on current political events.

7 Asia yearbook.

Far Eastern Economic Review.   Hong Kong: The Author, 1961-, annual.

Includes a four-page survey on Macau which discusses political and economic events which occurred during the previous year. The text is more narrative and less geographical, historical and statistical than the *Europa year book* (q.v.) entry on Macau.

8 Macau.

Cesar Guillen-Nuñez.   Hong Kong: Oxford University Press, 1984. 68p. 2 maps. bibliog. (Images of Asia).

This general introduction to Macau, with emphasis on architecture, art, history and geography, is accompanied by twenty-eight plates. Art objects, paintings and historic buildings are illustrated.

9 Macau: a mais antiga colónia europeia no Extremo-Oriente.

(Macau: the oldest European colony in East Asia.)
Jaime do Inso.   Macau: Tipografia do Orfanato do Imaculada Conceição, 1930. 152p. bibliog.

Despite a large number of typographical errors, this book contains information on the geography, economy, and politics of Macau in the 1920s which is usually difficult to find. Also included are chapters on the Portuguese communities in East Asia and the Portuguese missions in China as well as many old photographs.

10 **Macau.**
Edited by the Hongkong and Shanghai Banking Corporation. Hong
Kong: The Author, 1987. 3rd ed. 39p. 2 maps. (Hongkong and Shanghai
Banking Corporation Business Profile Series).
A general background is followed by sections on economics, statistics and business.
Residential information and a guide to the location of the Hongkong Bank group
offices are also supplied.

11 **Macau.**
Frank H.H. King. In: *The Far East and Australasia*. London: Europa,
1989. 20th ed. p. 622–29.
This guide, which is published annually, includes a concise, detailed and up-to-date
review of Macau. Emphasis is on legal, political and economic matters. The 1989
edition contains an appended statistical survey and a directory of various government
and media organizations.

12 **Ou Mun Kwu Kâm. (Aòmén gǔjīn.)** (Macau yesterday and today.)
Lei P'áng Chü (Lǐ Péngzhu). Hong Kong: Sānlián Shūlián; Macau:
Xīngguāng Chūbǎnshè, 1988. 250p.
Short sketches of places and events in Macau, past and present, are combined to
present a general introduction to Macau.

13 **Macau souvenir.**
[Comissão de Turismo]. Macau: [The Author], (ca. 1938). [n.p.]
Presents a collection of twenty-four black-and-white plates of famous landmarks with a
comment on each in Portuguese, English, and Chinese.

14 **Macao: A handbook.**
Macao Harbour Works Department. Macau: The Author, 1926. 41p.
map.
Presents a delightful look at the Macau of 1925 through the eyes of the government.
Besides details of history and geography, lists of various businesses are appended.

15 **The renascence of Macao.**
Francisco Monteiro. Macau: Direcção das Obras dos Portos,
(ca. 1924). 86p.
Provides an overly optimistic description of the territory's geography, economy, and
future potential for development. The most enjoyable parts are the sixty-seven old
photographs accompanied by detailed descriptions of parts of the city.

16 **The statesman's year-book.**
Edited by John Paxton. London: Macmillan, 1984-. annual.
Offers a brief survey on Macau which is appended to the entry on Portugal (in the
1987-88 edition, p.1011-13) listing vital statistics and providing notes on history and
politics.

17 **Macau a glimpse of glory: Macau um vislumbre de glória.**
Harry Rolnick. Hong Kong: Ted Thomas, [n.d.] [94p].
Presents a walk around the territory with colour photographs. The text is in English, Portuguese and Chinese.

18 **Asia & Pacific review.**
World of Information. Saffron Walden, England: The Author, 1979-. annual.
Recent issues have included three-page surveys of Macau (in the 1988 edition, p. 132-34) concentrating on recent political events, economics, and tips for the business traveller.

Macao.
See item no. 207.

Geography and Geology

General and physical

19 **Geologia da Província de Macau.** (A geology of the Province of Macau.)
João Carríngton Simões da Costa.   Oporto, Portugal: Sociedad
Geológica de Portugal, 1944. 43p. map. bibliog.
Presents a discussion of the rock types found in Macau (mostly granitic and basaltic).
Analysis of rocks found in southern China is used to complement Macau data.
Carríngton da Costa concludes that the Macau peninsula was once an island, but
sediments from the Pearl River connected Macau with the Chinese mainland, perhaps
around the time of the arrival of the Portuguese in the 16th century.

20 **Fisiografia e geologia da Província de Macau.** (A physical geography and
geology of the Province of Macau.)
João Carríngton Simões da Costa, M. J. Lemos de Sousa.   Macau:
Imprensa Nacional, 1964. 50p. map. bibliog.
This book represents the most recent general geology of Macau. After a geographical
introduction, there follows a substantial geological and geomorphological description
of Macau. The map accompanying the text contains some errors in geological
identification. In addition, there are thirty-three black-and-white photographs of
geomorphological features and geological aspects.

21 **Macau: imagens e números.** (Macau: images and numbers.)
António Costa.   Lisbon: Centro de Estudos Geográficos, 1981-82.
2 vols. 42 maps. bibliog. (Estudos de Geografia das Regiões Tropicais).
These volumes, produced by the Linha de Acção, represent the only complete
geography of Macau. Volume one (with sixty-two pages) concentrates on physical
geography and volume two (with 119 pages) discusses human geography. Much of the
material is drawn from secondary sources. The text is well-illustrated, although of off-
print quality. The statistical data covers the years 1970 to 1979.

5

Geography and Geology. General and physical

22 **Development of Macau's city landscape.**
Craig Duncan. In: *Macau: city of commerce and culture.* Edited by
Rolf Dieter Cremer. Hong Kong: UEA Press, 1987, p. 71–85. map.
bibliog.
Provides a general discussion of Macau's urban spread and contemporary urban
patterns. Some emphasis is given to housing conditions and traffic problems.

23 **Notas científicas.** (Scientific notes.)
Macau, Serviço Meterológico. Macau: Imprensa Nacional, 1951-57.
irregular.
These notes are in English as well as Portuguese and give information on various
climatic topics. Subjects covered include humidity, forecasting, precipitation, wind
components, temperature, fog, and barometric tendency. In many cases statistical data
is included.

24 **Resultados dos observações meteorológicas de Macau.** (Results of
meteorological observations of Macau.)
Macau, Serviço Meteorológico. Macau: Imprensa Nacional, 1952-.
monthly.
Presents meteorological data in Portuguese and English. The data is broken down by
months.

25 **Uma rocha basáltica de Macau.** (A basaltic rock of Macau.)
J. M. Cotelo Neiva. Oporto, Portugal: Imprensa Moderna, 1946. 10p.
This microscopic and chemical analysis of a rock found at the base of São Francisco
Hill on the Macau peninsula was first published in the Boletim da Sociedade Geológica
de Portugal, vol. 5, no. 3. (1946). Neiva concludes that this basaltic rock is the volcanic
equivalent of a troctolite and names it *macauite*. The piece includes a resumé in
French.

26 **Rochas eruptivas da península de Macau e das ilhas de Taipa e Coloane.**
(Effusive rocks from the peninsula of Macau and the islands of Taipa
and Coloane.)
J. M. Cotelo Neiva. Oporto, Portugal: Sociedade Geológica de
Portugal, 1944. 40p.
This article, which was originally published in the Boletim da Sociedade Geológica de
Portugal, vol. 3, no. 3 (1944), describes both macroscopically and microsopically
various effusive rocks from the peninsula, Coloane and Taipa. Types analyzed include
biotite granites, granitic aplites, pegmatites, olivine basalts, microgranites and
andesites. In conclusion the various characteristics of each type are summarized.

27 **O maior tufão de Macau: 22 e 23 de Setembro de 1874.** (The greatest
typhoon in Macau 22 to 23 September, 1874.)
Manuel Teixeira.   Macau: Tipografia da Missão do Padroado, 1974.
50p.
Discusses the origin of the word, *tufão*, and the signs which are believed, in Macau, to
indicate that a typhoon is coming. Teixeira relates the damage done by the terrible
typhoon which hit in 1874, drawing on various government documents issued at that
time.

28 **Aòmén jìlüè.** (Topography of Macau.)
Compiled by Yìn Guāngrèn, Zhāng Rǔlín.   Woodblock print of 1751.
2 vols. 9 maps.
This traditional Chinese gazetteer is divided into two volumes with forty-nine and fifty-
nine Chinese-style pages respectively. The work concentrates on the geography,
administration and Portuguese customs of Macau. A copy of the topography is held in
the library of the School of Oriental and African Studies in London and the text was
translated into Portuguese by Luís Gonzaga Gomes *Ou-Mun-Kei-Leok: Monografia de
Macau* (Macau: Imprensa Nacional, 1950).

**La découverte de la Chine par les Portugais au XVIème siècle et la
cartographie des Portulans.** (The discovery of China by the Portuguese in the
16th century and the cartography of the Portulans.)
See item no. 100.

Macao: the holy city: the gem of the orient earth.
See item no. 77.

Imagens de Macau. (Images of Macau.)
See item no. 3.

Political and economic geography

29 **The first land use map of Macau.**
Chiu Tse-Nang.   *Hong Kong Geographical Association Bulletin*, no. 5
(March 1975), p. 31-39. 4 maps. bibliog.
As a result of his land use survey of Macau in 1972, Dr. Chiu produced a map which
he claims to be the first land use map of Macau, at least in English. The land use
classification for the Macau peninsula employed nine categories, modified from the
scheme employed by the planning branch of the Public Works Department of the
Hong Kong government. This classification became the basis for a 1983 comparative
survey undertaken by Richard Louis Edmonds in 'Land use in Macau: changes
between 1972 and 1983' (q.v.). Chiu describes changes he found between 1962 and

Geography and Geology. Political and economic geography

1972. The 1962 data is based on an 'occupancy' map found in Raquel Soeiro de Brito's *Imagens de Macau* (Images of Macau) (q.v.), p. 21.

30 **Industrial plant location in the territory of Macau.**
Craig Duncan. *Asian Geographer*, vol. 5, no. 1 (1986), p. 61-77. map.
Following a discussion of plant location theory is a description of industries found in Macau and a classification of industrial regions.

31 **Land use in Macau: changes between 1972 and 1983.**
Richard Louis Edmonds. *Land Use Policy*, vol. 3, no. 1 (Jan. 1986), p. 47-63. 10 maps.
A general introduction to Macau is followed by a description of reconstructed land use maps for 1946 and 1962. Separate land use maps of the Macau peninsula, Taipa, and Coloane for 1972 and 1983 are presented and changes are discussed. It is demonstrated that agricultural land has decreased whereas commercial, residential, and industrial land use has increased. Finally, future plans for the territory up to ca. 2000 AD are discussed.

32 **Aòmén.** (Macao.)
Miao Hungkee, Ho Taichang, Léi Qiáng, Zhèng Tiānxiáng, Wong Chousun. Guangzhou, China: Zhōngshān Dàxué Chūbǎnshè, 1988. 230p. 18 maps. bibliog.
This is the most up-to-date human geography of Macau in Chinese. The authors have relied solely on Chinese and English language material. One chapter is devoted to physical geography.

33 **Breve memória documentada acêrca do território neutro situado entre a peninsula de Macau e o território da sub-prefeitura da Chin-San.** (A brief documented paper concerning the neutral territory situated between the peninsula of Macau and the territory of the subprefecture of Qianshan.) Govêrno da Província de Macau, José Luis Marques. Macau: Imprensa Nacional, 1923. 7p.
A note requesting that the neutral territory between the Macau peninsula and China be extended on the Chinese side to the nearest hilltops. This paper is one of a series including the three following texts also by the Govêrno da Província de Macau and José Luis Marques: *Breve memória documentada acêrca da soberania e jurisdição de Portugal na Taipa* (A brief documented paper concerning the sovereignty and jurisdiction of Portugal on Taipa) (Imprensa Nacional, 1923. 17p); *Breve memória documentada acêrca da soberania e jurisdição de Portugal na Ilha de D. João, Macarira ou Sio-Vong-Cam* (A brief documented paper concerning the sovereignty and jurisdiction of Portugal on the Island of Dom João, Macarira or Sio-Vong-Cam) (Imprensa Nacional, 1923. 12p); and *Breve memória documentada acêrca da soberania e jurisdição de Portugal na 'Ilha da Lapa'* (A brief documented paper concerning the sovereignty and jurisdiction of Portugal on the 'Island of Lapa') (Imprensa Nacional, 1923. 20p.). Also in this series is a booklet probably written by Alfredo Rodrigues dos Santos, entitled, '*Breve memoria documentada acêrca do soberania de Portugal no 'Ilha Verde'.* (A brief documented paper concerning the sovereignty and jurisdiction of Portugal on Ilha Verde.) (Imprensa Nacional, 1922. 12p.). These papers state, in

8

rather emotional terms, the Portuguese claims to the surrounding islands which the Guangzhou Nationalist government was contesting. Today, Ilha Verde and Taipa are administered by Portugal whereas the other territories discussed in these papers are under Chinese administration. In the prologue to the paper concerning Dom João (Xiaohengqin Island), the author indicates that he was preparing similar papers concerning Coloane and Tai-Vong-Cam (Dahengqin) Islands. These papers are more valuable for their descriptions of the geography of the area in 1922 than for their diplomatic debate.

34 **Memoire sur la souveraineté territoriale du Portugal à Macao.** (A memorandum on the territorial sovereignty of Portugal in Macau.) [Noguiera Soares]. Lisbon: Imprimerie Nationale, 1882. 85p.

This booklet represents an attempt by the Portuguese government to present its case for the sovereignty of Macau at a time when Britain had gained full sovereignty over Hong Kong. A response, in part, to Sir Anders Ljungstedt's book, *An historical sketch of the Portuguese settlements in China and of the Roman Catholic Church and missions in China* (q.v.) which questioned the vagueness of Macau's status, the government argues that there is no evidence against Portuguese sovereignty since Portugal's occupation of Macau in the 16th century.

Relatório de execução do plano de investimentos (1983-1984): investment plan execution report (1983-1984).
See item no. 233.

Fortifications of Macau, their design and history.
See item no. 293.

Macau: relatório da Direcção dos Serviços das Obras Públicas 1932. (Macau: a report of the Directorate of the Public Works Department 1932.)
See item no. 241.

Maps, atlases and gazetteers

35 **The Island of Taipa, Macau: a land use and tourist map 1984.**
Edited by Richard Louis Edmonds, Chan See Chung. Hong Kong: The Author, 1984. 1 sheet map.

A single sheet map of the Island of Taipa at 1:8000 scale with an inset map of Taipa Village at 1:2000 scale. The maps show eleven land use categories, and include bus routes, restaurants, and a table of tourist information. The sheet is produced in four languages: Chinese, Portuguese, English, and Japanese with the only known Taipa street index on the back as well as a list of hotels.

36 **Toponímia de Macau.** (Macau place names.)
Manuel Teixeira. Macau: Imprensa Nacional, 1979, 1981. 2 vols.

Volume one, *Ruas com nomes genéricos.* (Streets with generic names.), contains a detailed description of all streets, excluding those named after individuals, grouped by various districts on the Macau peninsula and on Taipa and Coloane. In volume two, *Ruas com nomes de pessoas.* (Streets named after people.), the street names are categorized as Saints, governors, bishops and priests, teachers at the Liceu, historical and literary figures, and others. Name changes and historical references are included and a considerable number of black-and-white photographs are appended.

37 **Antigos navegadores e marinheiros ilustres nos monumentos e toponímia de Macau.** (Former famous navigators and sailors with monuments and place names in Macau.)
Macau: Serviços de Marinha, 1984. 17p. map.
Describes the monuments to Vasco de Gama, Jorge Álvares and João Maria Ferreira do Amaral. There are notes about the famous navigators after whom approximately thirty streets in Macau are named. An accompanying map shows the location of all these streets and monuments.

Flora da Ilha de Coloane. (Flora of Coloane Island.)
See item no. 61.

Flora da Ilha da Taipa: monografia e carta temática: Flora of Taipa Island: monography and thematic map.
See item no. 62.

Taipa e Coloane. (Taipa and Coloane.)
See item no. 147.

Tourism and travel guides

38 **Discovering Macau.**
John Clemens.   Hong Kong: Macmillan, 1983. 3rd ed. 152p.
5 maps. bibliog.
This is one of the few tour guides which is devoted solely to Macau. Besides the normal tourist information and historical background, there are walking tours and much detail about places to visit. Unfortunately, the book is weak on Taipa and Coloane.

39 **Hong Kong, Macau and Canton.**
Carol Clewlow.   Melbourne: Lonely Planet, 1981. 188p. 12 maps.
The Macau section is brief (p. 134-50) with an even briefer update on p. 185. The emphasis is on helping the traveller to keep costs down.

40 **Golden Guide to Hongkong and Macao.**
P. H. M. Jones.   Hong Kong: Far Eastern Economic Review, 1969.
432p. 6 maps. bibliog.
Although now outdated, the Macau section (p. 336-415) contains good historical description and thirty-three photographs. Perhaps because the author's wife is from

Geography and Geology. Tourism and travel guides

Macau, the territory is given better coverage than in most Hong Kong-Macau guidebooks.

41 **Hong Kong.**
Edited by Leonard Lueras, R. Ian Lloyd, Saul Lockhart. Hong Kong: Apa, 1988. 6th ed. 338p. 18 maps. bibliog. (Insight Guides).
Includes two sections on Macau: 'Macau' (p. 194-209) by Lockhart which is a general introduction, and 'Macau guide in brief' (p. 309-17) which contains plenty of useful information for the short-stay tourist. This guide is also available in French, Portuguese, German, Italian, and Spanish language editions.

42 **Macau travel trade handbook 88/89.**
Macau: Macau Government Tourist Office, 1988, 63p. 3 maps.
The official guidebook to Macau which is reissued annually and is a particularly good source for obtaining up-to-date price information on tours and hotels.

43 **Hong Kong, Macau and Taiwan.**
Nina Nelson. London: Batsford, 1984, 157p. 8 maps.
This travel guide devotes most space to Hong Kong (108 pages.) with the Macau chapter occupying only twenty-seven pages. Despite the superficiality of the Macau section, there is much information which could help in planning a trip.

44 **Papineau's guide to Hong Kong and spotlight on Macau.**
Edited by Aristide J. G. Papineau. Singapore: André, 1977. 9th ed. 215p. 3 maps.
The Macau section (p. 183-201) is a rather small spotlight. The guide contains general information which is concentrated on hotels and restaurants.

45 **à Hong-Kong, Macao, Singapour.** (To Hong Kong, Macau, and Singapore.)
Christine Routier-le Diraison. Paris: Hachette Guides Bleus, 1988, 126p. 7 maps.
Pages sixty-two to seventy-five provide general tourist information on the territory.

46 **Fodor's Hong Kong and Macau 1988.**
Edited by Jacqueline Russell, Saul Lockhart, Shann Davies, Harry Rolnick. London: Hodder & Stoughton, 1987. 292p. 9 maps.
Introductory chapters (p. 1-52) give general information on both Hong Kong and Macau with portions on Macau in the back of each chapter. At the end of this guidebook (p. 235-80) a substantial section on Macau by Davies includes an up-to-date restaurant guide.

47 **The Macau Mokes guide to Macau.**
Elizabeth M. Thomas. Macau: Macau Mokes, 1988, 56p. map. bibliog.
This up-to-date but brief guidebook offers hints on shopping and unusual facts. Includes many advertisements, a few recipes and a brief annotated bibliography.

11

48 **Ou Mun lôi yâu (Aòmén lǚyóu).** (Macau travel.)
    Ngâi Kóng (Yì Gāng.)   Macau: Xīngguāng Chūbǎnshè, 1987. 61p. map.
This general Chinese language guide includes a discussion of famous sites as well as lists of restaurants, hotels and night clubs. It is illustrated by many black-and-white photographs.

49 **Macao: une ville portugaise.** (Macau: a Portuguese city.)
    Lisbon: Agência Geral do Ultramar, [n.d.] 32p.
An outdated guidebook to the territory which provides a feel of Macau in the early 1950s.

50 **Macau Travel Talk.**
    Macau: Department of Tourism, Government of Macau, [1976]-. 2nd series. monthly.
Distributed through the Tourist Information Bureaux and hotels of Macau, this paper gives information about recent developments in Macau's tourist industry, as well as articles about specific sites in Macau, the history of the territory, and reviews of books on Macau.

51 **Macau Voyager.**
    Hong Kong: South China Morning Post, [1982-83] bi-monthly.
This bilingual magazine, written in English and Chinese, was distributed to passengers on their way to Macau from Hong Kong on the jetfoils of the Shun Tak group. It contains colour photographs and articles for tourists on Macau.

Viva Macau!
See item no. 2.

Macao.
See item no. 207.

The Island of Taipa, Macau: a land use and tourist map 1984: Mapa da Ilha da Taipa, Macau: utilização de terrenos e turismo.
See item no. 35.

Urban geography and planning

52 **Macau.**
    Craig Duncan.   *Cities*, vol. 3, no. 1 (Feb. 1986), p. 2-11. map.
A brief historical survey of Macau is followed by a sketch of plans for the city's future.

53 **The Macau city region, a priori urban concepts and Macau development.**
Craig Duncan.   In: *Resources and development of the Pearl River delta.*
Edited by Victor Feng Shuen Sit.   Hong Kong: Wide Angle Press,
1984. p. 149-64.
Begins by presenting Macau as a daily commuting region and then provides a brief
background on settlement history. The article defines the Macau peninsula as the 'built
urban area', Taipa as the 'peri-urban area', and Coloane as an 'immediate contact
hinterland'. The author contends that changes in Macau's urban fringe replicate
situations found within urban fringes elsewhere. Many of the changes planned in the
early 1980s are described in detail. Finally, the future for Macau as a major node for
development of the western Pearl River delta region is considered.

54 **Linhas de acção governativa, plano de investimentos: análise de situação
económica e financeira do Território.** (Lines of government action,
investment plan: an analysis of the economic and financial situation of
the Territory.)
Governo de Macau.   Macau: Imprensa Oficial, 1987. 258p.
A government publication containing a speech made by the Governor, Joaquim Pinto
Machado, when the 1987 budget was being presented to the Legislative Assembly and
three lengthy appendices describing detailed plans for investment and the budget
during 1987.

Housing in Macau.
See item no. 204

Environmental protection

55 **A arborização em Macau: intervenção de Tancredo do Casal Ribeiro
(1883-1885).** (Afforestation in Macau: the intervention of Tancredo do
Casal Ribeiro (1883-1885).
António Júlio Emerenciano Estácio.   Macau: Serviços Florestais e
Agrícolas, 1985. 27p. bibliog.
Pays a tribute to Tancredo Caldeira do Casal Ribeiro who was in charge of the
afforestation of Guia Hill on the Macau peninsula from 1883 to 1885.

56 **Dinâmica das zonas verdes na cidade de Macau.** (The dynamics of the
green zones in the city of Macau.)
António Júlio Emerenciano Estácio.   Macau: Serviços Florestais e
Agrícolas, 1982. 60p. 4 maps. bibliog.
Argues for the preservation of greenery in Macau. This well illustrated book discusses
the problems of building development which is destroying vegetation and trees whose
roots have been cemented in by road development. Many photographs compare the
luscious vegetation of Macau's streets in the past with the sparser reality of today.

Flora and Fauna

57 **Contribuição para o estudos da flora médica macaense.** (A contribution towards the study of Macaense medical flora.)
Ana Maria de Sousa Marques da Silva Amaro.   Macau: Imprensa Nacional, 1965. 16p. (*Boletim do Instituto Luís de Camões*, no. 1).
Provides a résumé of the medicinal uses of the various members of the rutaceae family found in Macau. A total of eleven plants are introduced with their Latin, Portuguese, Cantonese, and Macaense names.

58 **Espécies botânicas goesas da flora Macau.** (Goan botanical species amongst the flora of Macau.)
Ana Maria de Sousa Marques da Silva Amaro.   Macau: Imprensa Nacional, 1966. 22p. (*Boletim do Instituto Luís de Camões*, no. 2).
This pamphlet lists twelve species of flora introduced to Macau from Goa over the centuries and discusses their uses in both countries. The author states that there are probably a hundred such species, the most famous being mango, but selects the twelve most common, giving their names in Latin, Portuguese, Goan and the Macaense dialects of Portuguese, Concanim, and Cantonese.

59 **Guia ilustrado de cobras venenosas de Macau e das Ilhas da Taipa e Coloane.** (An illustrated guide to venomous snakes of Macau and the Islands of Taipa and Coloane.)
Leonel Zilhão A. S. Barros.   Macau: Centro de Informação e Turismo, 1978. 48p. map.
A discussion of the half dozen venomous snakes found in the territory is followed by a section of questions and answers about Macau snakes with an English translation.

60 **Manual de identificação das aves de Macau.** (An identification manual of the birds of Macau.)
Leonel Zilhão A. S. Barros.   Macau: Direcção dos Serviços de Turismo, [1980]. 112p. 3 maps.
An initial section on birdwatching techniques (p. 14-51) is followed by descriptions of forty-five varieties of birds commonly seen in Macau. Migration habits are also discussed.

61 **Flora da Ilha de Coloane.** (Flora of Coloane Island.)
António Júlio Emerenciano Estácio, translated from the Portuguese by Lei Song Fan.   Macau: Serviços Florestais e Agrícolas, 1982. 59p. map. bibliog.
This well-illustrated booklet describes the eleven most common species of vegetation found on Macau's southernmost island. Also highlighted are eight special species and a 1.10,000 scale map shows the distribution of these species. The text is in Portuguese and Chinese.

62 **Flora da Ilha da Taipa: monografia e carta temática/ Flora of Taipa Island: monography and thematic map.**
António Júlio Emerenciano Estácio, translated from the Portuguese by Jorge Graca, Lei Song Fan.   Macau: Missão de Estudos Cartográficos, 1978. 31p. map.
Describes nine species of vegetation found on the island of Taipa with a map showing their distribution drawn at 1:7,500 scale. The descriptions of each species are in Portuguese, Chinese and English and each is several paragraphs long.

63 **Catálogo descritivo do 380 espécies botanicas da Colónia de Macau.** (A descriptive catalogue of 380 botanical species of the colony of Macau.)
Aires Carlos de Sá Nogueira.   Macau: Serviços Florestais e Agrícolas, 1984. 2nd ed. 176p.
Although dated (it was first published in 1933), this catalogue provides the most detailed account of species found in Macau. The text is Portuguese but Chinese and Latin names are provided as well as cross references to the same species in English and French books about the vegetation of Hong Kong and Indochina.

Dinâmica das zonas verdes na cidade de Macau. (The dynamics of the green zones in the city of Macau.)
See item no. 56.

15

Travellers' Accounts

Pre-1900

64   **The Suma Oriental of Tomé Pires and the book of Francisco Rodrigues.**
Edited by Armando Cortesão. London: Hakluyt Society, 1944. 2 vols.
511p. 43 maps. bibliog. 2nd series nos. XXXIX, XC.
An English translation accompanies the original Portuguese text of Tomé Pires'
account of places in Asia from the Red Sea to Japan written between 1512 and 1515.
Also included are translations of Francisco Rodrigues' rutter and almanack and maps
dating from before 1515. The *Suma Oriental*, written largely in Malacca, was the first
Portuguese account of China to reach Europe, but remained generally unknown until
its rediscovery by Armando Cortesão in Paris during the 1930s. There are no direct
accounts of the place where Macau now stands but some mention of the Pearl River
(Zhu Jiang) delta area. Similar information can be found in Armando Cortesão's
*Primeira embaixada europeia à China: o boticário e embaixador Tomé Pires e a sua
'Suma oriental'*. (The first embassy to China: the apothecary and ambassador Tomé
Pires and his 'Suma Oriental'.) (Lisbon: Seara Nova, 1945. 88p.)

65   **Jornada de Ántonio de Albuquerque Coelho.** (The journey of Ántonio de
Alburquerque Coelho.)
João Tavares de Vellez Guerreiro, preface by J. F. Marques Pereira.
Lisbon: Escriptorio, 1905. 165p. (Bibliotheca de Classicos Portuguezas).
Narrates the story of the voyage of Ántonio de Albuquerque Coelho, Governor and
Captain General of Macau, from Goa to Macau in 1718. Tavares de Vellez Guerreiro
was the captain who accompanied Albuquerque Coelho. This book, which can be
found in the library of the School of Oriental and African Studies, London, is only
recommended for specialists in this period of Portugal's colonial history.

66 A new account of the East Indies.
Alexander Hamilton. London: Argonaut, 1930. 2 vols. 10 maps.
The diary of a Scottish merchant, first published in Edinburgh in 1727. Hamilton sailed out of the Thames in 1688 for points east returning to London in 1725. In 1703-04, he arrived in the Macau area (vol. 2, p. 116-24) anchoring at Taipa to repair his vessel. There is also mention of Macau in relation to the building of a fort on Timor and to struggles with the Timorean people (vol. 2, p. 74).

67 Bits of old China.
William C. Hunter. London: Kegan Paul, Trench, 1885. 280p. map.
Portrays short sequences from the lives of Westerners in China from 1640 to 1842 along with some anecdotes about Chinese society. One chapter, 'Macao - Old Residents' (p. 147-61) contains general history mixed with a description of Macau and its foreign residents in the 1880s. The factual information contains many errors but the book is still very interesting reading.

68 The travels of Mundy in Europe and Asia, 1608-1667.
Peter Mundy, edited by Richard Carnac Temple. London: Hakluyt Society, 1919. 316p. 6 maps. 2nd series, no. XLV, vol. III, part 1.
This transcript of Peter Mundy's travels on Captain John Weddell's ill-fated expedition to China is one of the earliest English language accounts of Macau. The portions of Mundy's diary most concerned with Macau are the entries from 27th June 1637 (p. 158) to December 1637 (p. 301).

69 Travellers tales of the South China coast: Hong Kong, Canton, Macao.
Compiled by Michael Wise. Singapore: Times Books International, 1986. 256p. map.
Presents short sketches of incidents in Macau, Hong Kong, and Guangzhou with descriptions of the three places. The earliest sketch dates from 1816 and the last one portrays an escape from a Hong Kong prisoner of war camp during the Japanese occupation of World War II. The emphasis is on Western comments about the Cantonese.

Research on early explorers

70 South China in the sixteenth century: being the narratives of Galeote Pereira, Fr. Gaspar da Cruz, O.P., Fr. Martín de Rada, O.E.S.A. (1550-1575).
Edited by Charles Ralph Boxer. London: Hakluyt Society, 1953. 388p. 12 maps. bibliog. 2nd series, no. CVI.
Comprises three narratives describing South China: *Certain reports of China, learned through the Portugals there imprisoned, and chiefly by the relation of Galeote Pereira, a gentleman of good credit, that lay prisoner in that country many years,* written by the Portuguese Galeote Pereira around 1550; *Treatise in which the things of China are related at great length, with their particularities, as likewise of the kingdom of Ormuz* (1569), written by the Portuguese Dominican friar, Gaspar da Cruz; and the account of

Travellers' Accounts. Research on early explorers

the Spanish Augustinian friar, Martín de Rada, *Relación de las cosas de China que propriamente se llama taybin* (1575). The third text was translated by Boxer whereas the other two were edited versions of existing translations. In his introduction, Boxer gives some background to the Portuguese arrival in south China and to the founding of Macau.

71 **China landfall, 1513: Jorge Alvares' voyage to China.**
José Maria Braga.   Hong Kong: Karel Weiss, 1956. 117p. 3 maps. bibliog.

Relates the life of Jorge Álvares, the first Portuguese to touch land in China at the mouth of the Pearl River. There is a lengthy discussion of various early Portuguese texts relating to China. Much of the Chinese romanization in this book, however, is incorrect.

72 **The 'Tamão' of the Portuguese pioneers.**
José Maria Braga.   *T'ien Hsia Monthly*, vol. 8, no. 5 (May 1939), p. 420-32.

Offers a refutation of the proposal found in Sir Anders Ljungstedt's *An historical sketch of the Portuguese settlements in China and of the Roman Catholic Church and missions in China* (q.v.), that Tamão, where Jorge Álvares first touched Chinese soil, was on the northwest coast of Shangchuan Island. Braga produces documentation to verify Tamão as the modern Neilingding (Lintin) Island on the eastern side of the Pearl River delta.

73 **Em demanda do Caitaio: a viagem de Bento de Goes à China (1603-1607).**
(In search of Cathay: the voyage of Bento de Góis to China, 1603-07).
Eduardo Brazão.   Lisbon: Agência Geral do Ultramar, 1954. 100p. 2 maps.

The first three-quarters of this book describe the life of Marco Polo and the rise of Portugal to obtain the padroado (ecclesiastical patronage) of the missions in China. Bento de Góis was an Azorian who repented his wild life while in India and entered the Company of Jesus. He was sent to look for the Cathay of Polo and to find out whether it was the same as China. After travelling the land route through the Pamirs, Bento de Góis died in Suzhou (Jiuquan, Gansu province), knowing that Cathay and China were one.

74 **The grand peregrination: being the life and adventures of Fernão Mendes Pinto.**
Maurice Collis.   London: Faber & Faber, 1949. 302p. 2 maps. bibliog.

Presents a narrative account of Fernão Mendes Pinto's voyages as related in his book, *Peregrinação* (Lisbon: Pedro Crasbeec, 1614; Lisbon: Cosmopolis Editora, 1930). Macau is specifically mentioned in relation to Pinto's fourth visit to Japan when he touched at Portuguese bases in the Pearl River delta during 1555.

75 **Fernão Mendes Pinto: un précurseur de l'exotisme au XVIᵉ siècle.**
(Fernão Mendes Pinto: a pioneer of exoticism in the 16th century.)
G. Le Gentil. Paris: Hermann, 1947. 321p. bibliog.

A discussion of the geographic and ethnographic value of Fernão Mendes Pinto's *Peregrinção*. Gentil adopts the opinion that the *Peregrinação* is a novel and not an autobiography, partly because the listing of countries does not follow the chronology of the man's life. However, Pinto does use information from his own travels as well as assumed facts about various countries from Abyssinia to Japan. Places visited by Pinto included the Pearl River delta area of China during 1555.

76 **Portugal no tecto do mundo.** (Portugal on the roof of the world.)
Benjamim António Videira Pires. Macau: Instituto Cultural, 1988.
151p. 2 maps. bibliog.

Relates the 'discovery' of Tibet by Father António de Andrade and the journey of 'discovery' of 'Great Cathay' by Bento de Góis from Goa in modern India to Suzhou (Jiuquan, Gansu province) in China during the early 17th century.

The Western pioneers and their discovery of Macao.
See item no. 93.

La découverte de la Chine par les Portugais au XVIème siècle et la cartographie des Portulans. (The discovery of China by the Portuguese in the 16th century and the cartography of the Portulans.)
See item no. 100.

20th century

77 **Macao: the holy city: the gem of the orient earth.**
J. Dyer Ball. Canton, China: China Baptist Publication Society, 1905.
67p.

Provides a description of the geography, history, administration and buildings of Macau at the beginning of the 20th century. Neighbouring islands are also described. The text is full of errors but appended errata help to rectify many of them.

78 **Macau, terra nossa. Solar de Portugal no Oriente.** (Macau, our land. The sun of Portugal in the Orient.)
Afonso Correia. Macau: Imprensa Nacional. 1951. 262p.

A series of short sketches of Macau in the 1940s by a Portuguese resident. Contains an interesting note on the difference between the terms macanese and macaísta (maquista).

Travellers' Accounts. 20th century

79 **Thrilling cities.**
    Ian Fleming.   London: Reprint Society, 1964. 2nd ed. 221p.

Macau is one of the cities Fleming travelled to and wrote about for the *Sunday Times* during 1959 and 1960. His article is reproduced with some additions as chapter two in this book (p. 29-48). The emphasis is on gambling at the Hotel Central and a luncheon with Dr. Pedro José Lobo, the famous gold smuggler, radio station owner and politician.

80 **Of geisha and gangsters: notes, sketches, snapshots from the Far East.**
    Frederick Joss.   London: Odhams, 1962. 249p. 2 maps.

Chapter nine (p. 173-89), 'Macao: more than a sinner's paradise', describes Joss' seedy experiences in Macau during 1960-61. While some of his facts seem dubious, his experiences evoke a Macau no longer to be found.

81 **Hong Kong et Macao.** (Hong Kong and Macau.)
    Joseph Kessel.   Paris: Gallimard, 1975. 276p.

Presents stories from the author's travels in the 1950s. The Macau section (p. 157-276) emphasizes the poverty and gambling found in the city at that time.

82 **Asia's bright balconies: Hong Kong, Macao, Philippines.**
    Colin Simpson, Claire Simpson.   Sydney; London: Angus & Robertson, 1962. 240p. 4 maps.

Includes a tourist's description of Macau in the early 1960s (p. 119-73) with text by Colin Simpson and drawings by Claire Simpson. The first section (p. 121-44) is a historical summary relying heavily on Boxer's *Fidalgos in the Far East 1550-1770: fact and fancy in the history of Macao* (q.v.). The second section provides a more rounded view than that found in *Of geisha and gangsters: notes, sketches, snapshots from the Far East* (q.v.).

83 **Off to Asia: Singapore, Malaysia, Hong Kong, Macau.**
    Colin Simpson.   Sydney; London: Angus & Robertson, 1973. 211p. 5 maps, bibliog.

The chapter on Macau (p. 160-200) concentrates on where to eat, where to gamble, and the beaches of Coloane. Simpson concludes with a section on his experiences of the seedy side of the city.

Cartas de um commandante no Extremo Oriente. (Letters of a commandant in the far East.)
See item no. 103.

The renascence of Macao.
See item no. 15.

Travellers tales of the South China coast: Hong Kong, Canton, Macao.
See item no. 69.

20

History

History of the Portuguese in East Asia

84 **The Christian century in Japan 1549-1650.**
Charles Ralph Boxer. Berkeley; Los Angeles, California; London:
University of California Press, 1967. 2nd ed. 397p. 2 maps. bibliog.

Presents a detailed historical account of Portuguese involvement in early mission
efforts in Japan up to the *sakoku*, or virtual closing of Japan to foreign trade and
missionaries in 1633. Boxer stresses the dual nature of Portugal's early interest in
Japan from both religious and monetary standpoints. Although Macau is not the focus
of this volume, it puts the Macau-Nagasaki link in perspective.

85 **A fidalgo in the Far East, 1708-1726: Antonio de Albuquerque Coelho in
Macao.**
Charles Ralph Boxer. *Far Eastern Quarterly* (Menhasha, Wisconsin),
vol. 5, no. 4 (Aug. 1946), p. 387-410.

Recounts the romantic life of António de Albuquerque Coelho (ca. 1682-1745) who
arrived in Macau in 1708 and was Governor from 1718 until he left the territory in
1720. Boxer attempts to describe the city as Coelho would have seen it when first
arriving.

86 **Fidalgos in the Far East 1550-1770: fact and fancy in the history of
Macao.**
Charles Ralph Boxer.   The Hague: Martinus Nijhoff, 1948. 268p. map.
bibliog.

This classic book on the history of Macau contains perhaps more detail, especially
concerning the lives of various fidalgos, than the individual interested in a general
introduction might wish. Yet Boxer attempts to set right several misconceptions about
Macau which are still prevalent in the literature today and this book makes good
reading for anyone who has already read other introductory material on the city's early

21

history. Material on Goa, on other Portuguese settlements in Asia, and on relations with the Dutch, Japanese, Chinese, and English is so extensive that this book is better viewed as a history of the Portuguese in East Asia rather than simply as a history of Macau.

87 **Francisco Vieira de Figueiredo: a Portuguese merchant-adventurer in South East Asia, 1624-1667.**
Charles Ralph Boxer. Gravenhage, Netherlands: Martinus Nijhoff, 1967. 113p. bibliog. (Verhandelingen van het Koninklijk Instituut voor Taal-, Land- enVolkenkunde, part 52).
Relates the biography of this merchant-adventurer complete with appendices and a glossary of relevant documents and terms (p. 55-110). Boxer notes Vieira de Figueiredo's attempts to get ships into Macau during 1663-67 when the newly founded Qing dynasty blockaded the southeastern coastal provinces (p. 45-46.).

88 **Four centuries of Portuguese expansion, 1415-1825: a succinct survey.**
Charles Ralph Boxer. Berkeley; Los Angeles, California: University of California Press, 1969. 2nd ed. 1972. 93p. map. bibliog.
As the title implies, Boxer gives a succinct survey of Portuguese expansion and helps to put Macau into its proper colonial historical perspective.

89 **The great ship from Amacon: annals of Macao and the old Japan trade, 1555-1640.**
Charles Ralph Boxer. Macau: Instituto Cultural, Centro de Estudos Marítimos, 1988. 361p. map. bibliog.
This book was first published in 1959 by the Centro de Estudos Históricos Ultramarinos in Lisbon. The first 171 pages are a year-by-year account of the events concerning the ships sent from Macau to Japan laden with Chinese silks to exchange for silver. The emphasis is on economics rather than on the personalities involved as in the case of *Fidalgos in the Far East* (q.v.). The second part of the book is a collection of technical documents in Portuguese relating to this trade.

90 **A note on the triangular trade between Macao, Manila, and Nagasaki.**
Charles Ralph Boxer. *Terrae Incognitae*, vol. 17 (1985), p. 51-59.
Briefly describes the rôle of Macau in relation to Manila and their competition for the Japan trade during the period of the Spanish (Castilian) and Portuguese dual monarchy.

91 **The Portuguese seaborne empire, 1415-1825.**
Charles Ralph Boxer. London: Hutchinson, 1969. 378p. 7 maps. bibliog.
Presents a more detailed discussion of Portuguese colonial activity than that found in *Four centuries of Portuguese expansion* (q.v.). This book also tries to explain why the Portuguese empire was the last to give up its colonies in the 20th century. Although coverage of Macau is marginal, this book provides an excellent background to an understanding of the Portuguese attitude toward the territory.

92 **The Portuguese pioneers of Hong Kong: Pioneiros portuguesas de Hong Kong.**
J. P. Braga, preface by A. de O. Sales. Macau: Instituto Cultural, 1987. 2nd ed. 28p.
Discusses the rôle of the Portuguese in improving horticulture in Kowloon and Pokfulam during the late 19th century. This article was originally written in 1930.

93 **The Western pioneers and their discovery of Macao.**
José Maria Braga. *Boletim do Instituto Português de Hong Kong (Secção de História)*, vol. 2 (1949), p. 7-214. Reprinted, Macau: Imprensa Nacional, 1949. 160p.
The reasons for the expansion and contraction of Portuguese power in Asia dominate this book, with only the last third concerned with the establishment of Macau. The author offers critical comments on other books about Portuguese expansion and settlement of Macau. Early Portuguese political, economic and religious efforts in Asia are generally portrayed in a positive light.

94 **Apointamentos para a história das relações diplomáticas de Portugal com a China 1516-1753.** (Notes on the history of Portuguese diplomatic relations with China 1516-1753).
Eduardo Brazão. Lisbon: Agência Geral das Colónias, 1949. 211p.
Discusses the embassies to China of Tomé Pires (1515-24), Manuel de Saldanha (1667-70), Alexandre Metelo de Sousa e Meneses (1725-28), and Francisco de Assis Pacheco de Sampaio (1752-53) with numerous footnotes and appendices containing relevant documents for all except the de Saldanha mission. Macau figures prominently as all the embassies passed through the city.

95 **Sino-Portuguese trade from 1514 to 1644: a synthesis of Portuguese and Chinese sources.**
T'ien-tsê Chang (Zhāng Tiānzé). Leiden, Netherlands: E. J. Brill, 1969, 2nd ed. 141p. bibliog.
First published in 1933, with some corrections in this edition, this English language work uses Chinese and Portuguese as well as Dutch sources for the early history of the Portuguese in East Asia. The study is well-documented and includes a sketch of China's early maritime trade as well as material on the rise of Macau. There are discrepancies with later work, especially that of C. R. Boxer in *Fidalgos in the Far East* (q.v.). A detailed critique of this work has been produced by Paul Pelliot, *T'ong Pao*, vol. 31 (1935), p. 58-94 (q.v.).

96 **The third Portuguese empire 1825-1975: a study in economic imperialism.**
Gervase Clarence-Smith. Manchester, England: Manchester University Press, 1985. 223p. 8 maps. bibliog.
An economic history which covers the late Portuguese empire in great detail. Although direct references to Macau are few, the relationship of the territory to the Portuguese Empire in its later years is well portrayed.

97 **L'arrivée des Portugais en Chine.** (The arrival of the Portuguese in China.)
Henri Cordier. *T'oung Pao.* vol. 12 (1911), p. 483-543.

Traces the expansion of Portuguese power from the taking of Ceuta to the arrival of the Portuguese on the China coast. One chapter is concerned with the establishment of the Portuguese at Macau (p. 524-29). Cordier presents all the opinions of Western scholars concerning the founding of Macau along with some information from Chinese sources.

98 **From Portugal to Japan: Macau's place in the history of world trade.**
Rolf Dieter Cremer. In: *Macau: city of commerce and culture.* Edited by Rolf Dieter Cremer. Hong Kong: UEA Press, 1987, p. 23-37. bibliog.

Describes Chinese international trade prior to the arrival of the Portuguese and traces Portugal's rise to commercial power. Cremer stresses the complementary nature of the two nations' economic policies at the time of the Portuguese arrival on the South China coast in the 16th century.

99 **Efemérides da história de Macau.** (An almanac of the history of Macau.)
Luís Gonzaga Gomes. Macau: Notícias de Macau, 1954. 267p.
(Colecção *Notícias de Macau*, no. XII).

This chronological register of past events relating to the Portuguese in Asia is arranged by days of the month. Events included range from the late 16th century to 1950.

100 **La découverte de la Chine par les Portugais au XVIème siècle et la cartgographie des Portulans.** (The discovery of China by the Portuguese in the 16th century and the cartography of the Portulans.)
Albert Kammerer. Leiden, Netherlands: E. J. Brill, 1944 229p. 15 maps.

An often cited pioneering work which was also published as a supplement to *T'oung Pao*, vol. 39. Assesses Portuguese contributions to the geographical knowledge of the Chinese coast. The first section reviews the achievements of the famous early Portuguese explorers; the location of Veniaga Island, Tamão or Tunmen (modern Neilingding Island, often called Lintin, in Guangdong province) where the Portuguese first traded directly with China; the impact of Portuguese trade at Liampo (Zhenhai near Ningbo in Zhejiang province) in the 1540s; the location of Shangchuan Island (in Guangdong province) where Saint Francis Xavier died in 1552; the location of Lampacau (according to Kammerer just to the west of Macau) where the Portuguese traded before moving to Macau in the 1550s; and the identification of the Zayton of Marco Polo as Quanzhou in Fujian province. The development of Macau up to 1650 is discussed in considerable detail on pages 106-44. The text has many footnotes.

101 **The relations between Portugal and Japan.**
Matsuda Kiichi. Lisbon: Junta de Investigações de Ultramar, Centro de Estudos Históricos Ultramarinos, 1965. 107p. bibliog.

Examines Portuguese-Japanese relations from around 1542 to the breakdown of relations in the mid-17th century, with a brief note about development since their resumption in 1860. The influence of Portugal on Japanese civilization is discussed in part two with emphasis on the printing industry.

102 **A embaixada de Manuel de Saldanha ao Imperador K'hang hi em 1667-1670 (subsídios para a história de Macau).** (The embassy of Manuel de Saldanha to the Kangxi Emperior in 1667-1670; a contribution to the history of Macau.)
Durval R. Pires de Lima. Lisbon: Tipografia e Papelaria Carmona, 1930. 23p.
Narrates Manuel de Saldanha's voyage to Goa, Macau and Beijing with comments on Macau's early relations with China and Japan.

103 **Cartas de um commandante no Extremo Oriente.** (Letters of a commandant in the Far East.)
Pedro Fragoso de Matos. Macau: Instituto Cultural, Serviços de Marinha, 1987. 195p. 4 maps.
Presents the notes of the commander of the *Gonçalves Zarco* which left Lisbon in 1960 and arrived in Macau in 1961 and again in 1962. The commander records his impressions of Macau as well as Hong Kong, Timor and other points in Asia and Africa.

104 **Un ouvrage sur les premiers temps de Macao.** (A work on the first days of Macau.)
Paul Pelliot. *T'oung Pao*, vol. 31 (1935), p. 58-94.
Provides a detailed, page-by-page critique of Chang T'ien-tsê's book, *Sino-Portuguese trade from 1514 to 1644: a synthesis of Portuguese and Chinese sources* (q.v.).

105 **A embaixada Mártir.** (The Mártir embassy).
Benjamim Videira Pires. Macau: Instituto Cultural, 1988. 2nd ed.
Relates the story of the embassy from Macau to Japan in 1640. This embassy was composed of sixty-one persons who were executed by the Japanese and subsequently beatified and canonized.

106 **Portugal in China.** (Portugal in China.)
Roderich Ptak. Bad Boll, GFR: Klemmerberg, 1980. 106p. 5 maps. bibliog.
Narrates the history of the arrival of the Portuguese in East Asia and their establishment of Macau, covering the period from the beginning of the 16th century to the mid-17th century.

107 **Jorge Álvares (quadros da sua biografia no Oriente).** (Jorge Álvares: sketches of his biography in the Orient.)
Artur Basílio de Sá. Lisbon: Agência Geral do Ultramar, 1956. 143p. bibliog.
This biography of the first Portuguese to reach China by sea via Malacca in 1553 is largely composed of primary documents.

108 **Os Portugueses na China.** (The Portuguese in China.)
     Salvador Saboya. Lisbon: Editorial Labor, 1938. 147p.

Chapters introducing the country of China, the efforts of the Jesuits in China, and the early history of the Portuguese embassies to China are followed by a chapter on Macau which places Portugal's position in the colony in a most favourable light. Finally, there is a brief note on the war between China and Japan which began in 1937 and in which the author clearly supports China. This book is for those who wish to read a somewhat emotional account of Portugal's 'glories' in East Asia when it was still fasionable to write in that vein.

109 **The survival of empire: Portuguese trade and society in China and the South China Sea, 1630-1754.**
     George Bryan Souza. Cambridge, England: Cambridge University Press, 1986. 230p. 9 maps. bibliog.

As the title implies, the emphasis is on economic links between Macau, other Portuguese settlements, and various ports from India to Japan. This scholarly text contrasts the rôle of the Portuguese crown with that of the local mestiço/casado populations in the maintenance of the Portuguese empire against Dutch, Chinese, Indian, English, and local Southeast Asian competition.

110 **India, Macau, Timor e a língua portuguesa** (India, Macau, Timor and the Portuguese language)
     Manuel Maria Variz. Vila Real, Portugal: Minerva Transmontana, 1978. 123p. bibliog.

Sings the praises of Portugal and God in Asia. Macau is covered in one chapter (p. 61-71) and a list of Governors is supplied (p. 73-78). The 1966-67 Taipa school incident is treated in considerable detail.

111 **Presença portuguesa no Extremo Oriente.** (The Portuguese presence in East Asia.)
     Macau: Instituto Cultural, 1986. 88p.

Presents papers given at a conference of the same title in Macau during 1983. The papers discuss Macau's history; Portuguese cultural impact upon Japan and Timor; the future of the Portuguese language in Asia; and the origin of Macau's currency, the pataca.

A política europeia no Extremo Oriente no século XIX e as nossas relações diplomáticas com a China. (European politics in the Far East in the 19th century and our diplomatic relations with China.)
See item no. 222.

History of Macau

112 **Dares-e-tomares nas relações luso-chinesas os séculos XVII e XVIII**
     através de Macau. (Ups and downs in Luso-Chinese relations during
     the 17th and 18th centuries over Macau.)
     Charles Ralph Boxer. *Arquivos de Macau: Boletim do Arquivo*
     Histórico de Macau, vol. 1 (Jan. 1981), 13p.
An off-print of this article was published by the Imprensa Nacional of Macau in 1981.
Boxer sees Sino-Portuguese relations as being at their most interesting during the 17th
and 18th centuries because of several topics: the lack of Portuguese women in Macau
for marriage; the territory's mixed Luso-Chinese jurisdiction; and the religious conflict
in Macau during this period. This paper represents a condensed form of Boxer's
thoughts on Macau.

113 **Macao as a religious and commercial entrepôt in the 16th and 17th**
     centuries.
     Charles Ralph Boxer. *Acta Asiatica*, vol. 26 (1974), p. 64-90.
This article divides the early history of Macau into three periods: 'The Japan trade
cycle, 1557-1640'; 'The years of crises, 1640-1670'; and 'Macao preserved and the
"dream of Japan," 1671-1700'. There is emphasis on contacts with Nagasaki and
Manila. The concentration on Japan may be due to the fact that this paper was first
given as a lecture at the International House of Japan in 1973. A Japanese translation
can be found in *Tōhōgaku*, no. 46 (July 1973).

114 **Murder most foul (a tragedy of old Macau in 1643).**
     Charles Ralph Boxer. *Mosaico*, vol. 1, no. 4 (Dec. 1950), 17p.
Notes the cruel acts committed by the Captain-General Dom Sebastian Lobo da
Silveira against the Portuguese and Spanish garrisons and his murder of the
Administrator of Crown Funds in Macau, Diogo Vaz Freire. This article was reissued
as an off-print by the Macao Cultural Circle in 1951.

115 **Portuguese society in the tropics.**
     Charles Ralph Boxer.   Madison; Milwaukee, Wisconsin: University of
     Wisconsin Press, 1965. 149p. 4 maps. bibliog.
The subtitle of this book is *The Municipal Councils of Goa, Macao, Bahia, and*
Luanda 1510-1800. Originally, Boxer gave four lectures on each of these cities at the
University of Wisconsin in 1964. The chapter on Macau (p. 42-71) traces the origins of
the Municipal Council. Boxer feels that the Municipal Council of Macau was the most
important of all the Portuguese colonial municipalities during the period covered.

116 **Seventeenth century Macau in contemporary documents and illustrations.**
Edited and translated by Charles Ralph Boxer.   Hong Kong: Heinemann (Asia), 1984. 184p. bibliog.

An updated collection of descriptions and documents written during the 1630s and 1640s which was first published in a 1942 Portuguese/English edition of 500 copies. The initial part contains three descriptions of Macau written between 1635 and 1638. Part two contains extracts from contemporary documents concerning the voyage of António Fialho Ferreira to Macau (1639-44) to inform the city of the restoration of the Portuguese crown after sixty years of Spanish rule.

117 **A voz do passado.** (The voice of the past.)
Jack [José] Maria Braga.   Macau: Instituto Cultural, 1987. 2nd ed. 78p.

Reproduces the *Colecção de varios factos acontecidos nesta mui nobre Cidade de Macau pelo decurso dos annos*, a document discovered by Braga in Portugal which discusses important dates related to Macau between 1552 and 1748. The period 1702-48 includes much information about community activities.

118 **Macau: cidade do nome de Deus na China, não há outra mais leal.**
(Macau: the city of the name of God in China, there is none other more loyal.)
Eduardo Brazão.   Lisbon: Agência Geral do Ultramar, 1957. 267p.
(Monografias dos Territórios do Ultramar).

In this orthodox Portuguese history of Macau for the 1950s, Brazão discusses the development of the territory from the 1550s to 1887. The appendix contains twenty-seven black-and-white sketches of Macau and south China and documents dating from 1643 on the proclamation of King Dom João in Macau. Abstracts in French and English are provided.

119 **A Macao narrative.**
Austin Coates.   Hong Kong: Oxford University Press, 1987. 2nd ed. 112p. bibliog.

A narrative history of early Portuguese settlement on the China coast, first published in 1978 by Heinemann in Hong Kong. This well-illustrated book includes anecdotes of major events in Macau's past and some brief comments on the city today. Coates stresses the impact of British policy on the fate of the territory.

120 **Resumo da história de Macau.** (An outline history of Macau.)
Eudore de Colomban.   Macau: Tipografia Mandarin, 1980. 3rd ed. 127p.

Despite some errors, this text, which dates from 1927, provides a succinct history of Macau from the early 16th century onwards. Useful as a quick reference work, for many years this was a standard textbook for students in Macau and its impact has been far-reaching. However, because of some factual errors and a lack of references, this book should be used with some caution. Eudore de Colomban was the pen name of Regis Gervaix.

121 **Macau entre dois tratados com a China 1862-1887.** (Macau between two treaties with China: 1862-1887.)
Lourenço Maria da Conceição. Macau: Instituto Cultural, 1988. 179p. bibliog.

The basic argument is that the treaty of 1887 between Portugal and China was not an 'unequal treaty' pressed upon China by Portugal but a treaty 'brought forth for the conveniences of China herself'. The author discusses the treaty of 1862 between Portugal and China, the operation of the Chinese customs in Macau, the coolie trade via Macau and its abolition and the treaty of 1887. In 1887, the Portuguese finally gave in on their claims to Wanzhai Island and, to a certain degree, on a Chinese fiscal post in the city, but gained sovereignty over Macau.

122 **Fragrant harbour: a short history of Hong Kong.**
G. B. Endacott, A. Hinton. Hong Kong: Oxford University Press, 1962. 196p. 4 maps. bibliog.

A useful historical survey of Macau appears in Appendix A (p. 197-203), 'The story of Macao'.

123 **Aòmén sìbǎinián.** (Macau, four hundred years.)
Fèi Chéngkāng, preface by Chén Xúlù' Shanghai China: Rénmín Chūbǎnshè, 1988, 431p.

This complete history of Macau, based on Chinese language sources available in the People's Republic of China, is divided into chronological sections.

124 **Historic Macao.**
Carlos Augusto Montalto de Jesus. Hong Kong: Oxford University Press, 1984. 2nd ed. 515p. map.

First published in 1926, this major history covers the development of Portuguese settlement on the China coast from its beginnings in the 16th century to the early 20th century. The author tries to demonstrate that Portuguese settlement in Macau was at the invitation of the Chinese and not merely an encroachment upon Chinese territory. The rise of Hong Kong is seen as the major reason for Macau's economic decline. Chapters added to the 1926 edition by Montalto de Jesus, suggest that Portugal was no longer able to govern the colony properly and that Macau should have been put under League of Nations administration.

125 **Contribution to an historical sketch of the Portuguese settlements in China, principally of Macao, and of the Portuguese envoys and ambassadors to China, of the Roman Catholic mission in China and of the Papal legates to China.**
Andrew Ljungstedt. Macau: [n.p.], 1832. 174p.

Argues the case against the Portuguese right of sovereignty in Macau. This text was the forerunner of the famous *An historical sketch of the Portuguese settlements in China and of the Roman Catholic Church and missions in China* (q.v.). Sir Anders Ljungstedt does not present the Portuguese presence in Macau in a favourable light. The latter half of the book is concerned with Portugal's political and religious activities in China.

126   **An historical sketch of the Portuguese settlements in China; and of the Roman Catholic Church and missions in China.**
Andrew Ljungstedt.   Boston, Massachussetts: James Munroe, 1836. 323p. 3 maps.

This is an updated version of the 1832 volume *Contribution to an historical sketch of the Portuguese settlements in China, principally of Macao, and of the Portuguese envoys and ambassadors to China, of the Roman Catholic mission in China and of the Papal legates to China* (q.v.). A discussion of Portuguese settlements before Macau is followed by a detailed analysis of the development of Macau and a discussion of Catholic missions in China. There is an appendix on the city of Guangzhou and the population and government of Macau are described in detail. Although there are mistakes in the historical interpretation, this book is a must for the serious student of Macau's history.

127   **Historical traces of Sun Yat-Sen's activities in Hong Kong, Macao and overseas.**
Edited by Ng Lun Ngai-ha, Chen Shenglin, Guo Jingrong, Luo Lixin. Hong Kong: Chinese University of Hong Kong; Guangzhou, China: Zhongshan University, 1986. 182p. 8 maps.

Written in English and Chinese, this book contains photographs of modern places in Macau where the Chinese revolutionary Sun Yat-sen was active.

128   **The demography of old Macau, 1555-1640.**
Roderich Ptak.   *Ming Studies*, no. 15 (Fall 1982), p. 27-35. bibliog.

The author has gathered considerable population data for early Macau. Despite the lack of a complete data set, his conclusion is that demographic changes were the result of export-led growth.

129   **Os extremos conciliam-se (transculturação em Macau).** (The extremes harmonize themselves: cultural interchange in Macau.)
Benjamim António Videira Pires.   Macau: Instituto Cultural, 1988. 215p.

A collection of essays describing various aspects of Macau but concentrating on how the city has served as a point of cultural interchange between Portugal and China. The early chapters deal with the beginnings of East Asia-European contact. Later chapters relate aspects of life in Macau during the past 400 years with the final chapters discussing more recent history.

130   **Origins and early history of Macau.**
Benjamim António Videira Pires.   In: Macau: city of commerce and culture. Edited by Rolf Dieter Cremer. Hong Kong: UEA Press, 1987, p. 7-21. bibliog.

The author describes the establishment of the Portuguese at Macau and explains the rôle Macau played in the transmission of Western science to East Asia. Also included is a brief description of the development of Macau's school system and a discussion of contemporary scholars and artists.

131 **A viagem de comércio Macau-Manila nos séculos XVI à XIX.**
(Commercial voyages between Macau and Manila from the sixteenth to
the nineteenth centuries.)
Benjamim Antonio Videira Pires.   Macau: Centro de Estudos
Marítimos, 1987. 2nd ed. 120p.

Provides a detailed study of this significant trade route during the height of its
importance. Pires sees the Macau-Manila relationship as normally friendly but also as
reflecting the highs and lows of European politics and the commercial competition of
the European powers.

132 **Instrução para o bispo de Pequim e outros documentos para a história
de Macau.** (Instruction by the bishop of Beijing and other documents
for the history of Macau.)
Portugal, Ministério das Colónias, preface by Manuel Múrias.
Lisbon: Agência Geral das Colónias, 1943, 380p.

Reprints ninety-four documents from Macau, Goa and Lisbon dated between 1586
and 1781. All are relevant to the study of Macau.

133 **A presença de Portugal em Macau.** (The presence of Portugal in
Macau.)
António da Silva Rego.   Lisbon: Agência Geral das Colónias, 1946.
108p. bibliog.

This account is more a justification of Portugal's claim to Macau and of the
continuation of the Portuguese administration than a history of the Portuguese
presence in Macau.

134 **O comércio de escravos em Macau: The so called Portuguese slave trade
in Macao.**
Manuel Teixeira.   Macau: Imprensa Nacional, 1976. 97p. bibliog.

This bilingual text was originally published in the *Boletim do Instituto Luís de Camões*,
vol. X, nos. 1, 2. The Portuguese section (p. 1-75) is much more detailed than the
English. Teixeira discusses the slave trade in the Portuguese section, but concentrates
on the post-19th century coolie trade from Macau to Cuba and Peru in the English. He
defends the rôle of Macau and Portugal in the coolie trade as being neither as
significant nor as cruel as is often assumed.

135 **Galeria de Macaenses ilustres do século XIX.** (Illustrious Macaenses of
the 19th century.)
Manuel Teixeira.   Macau: Imprensa Nacional, 1942. 656p.

As only 500 copies were originally printed, it may be difficult to find this book. The
biographies of sixteen famous Macaense are found in this volume which was printed to
commemorate the 800th anniversary of the founding of Portugal and the 300th
anniversary of the restoration of the Portuguese crown after sixty years of Castilian
rule. Each entry begins with a detailed discussion of the individual's family.
Biographies of ecclesiastic Macaenses are excluded since they appeared in Teixeira's
Macau e a sua diocese (q.v.).

136 **Galeria de mulheres ilustres em Macau.** (Illustrious women in Macau.)
Manuel Teixeira. Macau: Centro de Informação e Turismo Imprensa
Nacional, 1974. 75p.

Presents sketches of the lives of sixteen famous women of Macau. Included are
Spanish, Japanese, Chinese, Russian, American, and Italian women as well as
Macaense and Portuguese.

137 **Leal Senado:** (The Loyal Senate.)
Manuel Teixeira. Macau: Leal Senado, [1973]. 24p.

A brief history of the Macau senate and its current building, illustrated with sixteen
black-and-white photographs.

138 **Macau através dos séculos.** (Macau through the centuries.)
Manuel Teixeira. Macau: Imprensa Nacional, 1977. 87p.

Drawing on diaries and correspondence, the author relates descriptions of Macau for
the following years: 1563, 1598-99, 1635-37, 1672, 1710, 1745, 1774, 1794, 1798, 1829-
33, 1840, 1853, 1858, 1878-80, 1901, 1919 and 1924.

139 **Macau no séc. XVIII.** (Macau in the 18th century.)
Manuel Teixeira. Macau: Imprensa Nacional, 1984. 750p.

Covers events in Macau from 1700 to 1799. Within each year the events are listed
chronologically and a name index is appended.

140 **Macau no séc. XVI.** (Macau in the 16th century.)
Manuel Teixeira. Macau: Direcção dos Serviços de Educação e
Cultura, 1981. 89p.

Offers a year-by-year coverage of events in Macau from 1505 to 1599 with an
introductory note plus a short section on the origin of the name of Macau.

141 **Macau no séc. XIX: visto por uma jovem americana.** (Macau in the 19th
century: as seen by a young American woman.)
Manuel Teixeira. Macau: Direcção dos Serviços de Educação e
Cultura, 1981. 59p.

Summarizes the account of Macau found in the diary of Harriet Low, an American
who lived in Macau from 1829-34.

142 **Marinheiros ilustres relacionados com Macau.** (Famous sailors
connected with Macau.)
Manuel Teixeira. Macau: Centro de Estudos Marítimos, 1988. 238p.

Presents brief histories of famous Portuguese navigators who had some connections
with Macau. Begins with Jorge Álvares, the first Portuguese to arrive on the south
China coast in the 16th century, and continues to the mid-20th century. An appendix
describes the Portuguese battle with pirates on Coloane in 1910.

143 **Miguel de Arriaga.** (Miguel de Arriaga.)
Manuel Teixeira.   Macau: Imprensa Nacional, 1966. 203p. bibliog.
Discusses the family background and historical events surrounding the life of the
ouvidor (special magistrate), Miguel de Arriaga Brum da Silveira (1776-1824) who
virtually ruled Macau from 1802 until his death. Among the topics covered are
Arriaga's rôle in the introduction of vaccine to Macau and China, his initiation of
scholarships for study in Portugal, and his part in the English occupation of the
territory. The defeat of the pirate, Kam Pau Sai, and the liberal movement in Macau
are also considered.

144 **Os militares em Macau.** (The military in Macau.)
Manuel Teixeira.   Macau: Comando Territorial Independente, 1976.
614p. map.
A history of military organizations published to commemorate the disbanding of the
Portuguese Comando Territorial Independente de Macau and its replacement in 1975
with the Forças de Segurança (Security Forces), composed of local Macau people. An
initial background chapter gives details of various versions of the origin of the name of
Macau. This is followed by chapters discussing the military and civil governments,
fortifications, and incidents in the military history of Macau.

145 **Os ouvidores em Macau.** (The ouvidores in Macau.)
Manuel Teixeira.   Macau: Imprensa Nacional, 1976. 206p.
Gives an account of the lives of selected ouvidores (special magistrates) from 1580 to
1838. After 1838, judges were appointed. Lists of procuradores (judges for the Chinese
appointed from 1582 to 1884) and other types of judges are appended. An English
version of the book was published in 1979 (Macau: Tipografia Mandarim).

146 **Pedro Nolasco da Silva.** (Pedro Nolasco da Silva.)
Manuel Teixeira.   Macau: Imprensa Nacional, 1942. 100p.
Relates the story of a famous Macaense educator and translator of Chinese who taught
at various schools in Macau and was superintendent of the Santa Casa de
Misericórdia. Details are given about his family and his many contributions to the
welfare of Macau. Pedro Nolasco da Silva (1842-1912) has been called the first
Portuguese sinologist.

147 **Taipa e Coloane.** (Taipa and Coloane.)
Manuel Teixeira.   Macau: Direcção dos Serviços de Educação e
Cultura, 1981. 187p.
This compendium of notes covers Taipa and Coloane as well as Xiaohengqin Island
(Dom João), which is now Chinese administered but has been claimed by Portugal in
the past. Topics mentioned include battles with pirates and the establishment of
schools and hospitals.

148 **A voz das pedras de Macau.** (The voice of the stones of Macau.)
Manuel Teixeira.   Macau: Imprensa Nacional, 1980. 324p.
Lists and discusses phrases engraved on tombs and buildings throughout Macau. This
text was first published in the *Boletim do Instituto Luís de Camões*, vol. 12, nos. 3, 4;
vol. 13, nos. 1, 4.

149 **A aclamação del Rei D. João IV em Macau (subsídios históricos e biográficos).** (The acclamation of King D. João IV in Macau: historical and biographical aids.)
Frazão de Vasconcellos. Lisbon: Agência Geral das Colónias, 1929, 55p.
Originally published in the *Boletim de Agência Geral das Colónias*, no. 53, this note on the proclamation of King D. João IV in 1642 is accompanied by biographical information on António Fialho Fereira, the man who was sent to make the proclamation. Excerpts from relevant documents are provided.

150 **Ou Mun si leók (Aòmén shǐlüè).** (A brief history of Macau.)
Yün Póng kin (Yüán Bāngjiàn), Yün Kwâi Sâu (Yüán Guìxiù). Hong Kong: Zhōngliú Chūbǎnshè, 1988. 330p.
This general history of Macau is based largely on Chinese language sources. A chronological table of events covering the period from 1152 to 1986 is included.

Aòmén jìlüè. (Topography of Macau.)
See item no. 28.

The beginnings of printing at Macau.
See item no. 334.

Camões em Macau: contribuições para o estudo do problema. (Camões in Macau: contributions to the study of the problem.)
See item no. 260.

Camões esteve em Macau. (Camões was in Macau.)
See item no. 261.

As Canossianas na Diocese de Macau: 1 centenário (1874-1974). (The Canossians in the Diocese of Macau; the first century (1874-1974).)
See item no. 194.

Os Chins de Macau. (The Chinese of Macau.)
See item no. 164.

The fourth centenary of Jesuits at Macao.
See item no. 196.

A história e os homens da primeira república democrática do Oriente: biologia e sociologia de uma ilha cívica. (A history of the people of the first democratic republic of the Orient: the biology and sociology of a civic island.)
See item no. 162.

A Igreja de S. Domingos e os Dominicanos em Macau. (The Church of São Domingos and the Dominicans in Macau.)
See item no. 182.

The international status of Macao before 1887.
See item no. 220.

Macao: a handbook.
See item no. 14.

O maior tufão de Macau: 22 e 23 Setembro de 1874. (The greatest typhoon in Macau: 22 to 23 September, 1874.)
See item no. 27.

Os médicos em Macau. (Doctors in Macau.)
See item no. 210.

Was Camoens ever in Macau?
See item no. 257.

The British in Macau

151 **A seller of 'sing-songs': a chapter in the foreign trade of China and Macao.**
José Maria Braga. *Journal of Oriental Studies*, vol. 6, nos. 1, 2 (1961-64), p. 61-108.
Concentrates on British trade with China via Macau. Events and aspects described include the trade in 'sing songs' (clocks); the fur trade; the 'Dadaloy' affair (the first ship expelled from Macau for privateering); and the rise of private merchants outside the East India Company, notably John Henry Cox. Cox's last will and testament are included in an appendix.

152 **Prelude to Hong Kong.**
Austin Coates.   London: Routledge & Kegan Paul, 1966. 224p. 2 maps. bibliog. (Reprinted as *Macao and the British 1637-1842: Prelude to Hong Kong*, Hong Kong: Oxford University Press 1989.)
Describes the rise of British power on the China coast from the arrival of Captain John Weddell at Macau in 1637 to the founding of Hong Kong in 1842. Uses historical documents to narrate specific events, most of which are important in the history of Macau. Some of the material for this book is based on oral rather than textual sources.

153 **Foreign mud.**
Maurice Collis.   London: Faber & Faber, 1946. 310p. 5 maps.
A discussion of the Guangzhou opium trade between 1832 and 1842 based on the records of the British government, the accounts of European missionaries and the archives of the firm of Jardine and Matheson. A description of Macau in the 1830s is given near the beginning of the book. Several famous prints of Macau are reproduced.

154 **The great within.**
    Maurice Collis. London: Faber & Faber, 1941. 342p. 3 maps. bibliog.
This book attempts to cover European-Chinese contacts from the late Ming dynasty (1368-1644) to the founding of the Chinese Republic in the early 20th century. A descriptive history, it contains accounts of visits by early British seamen to the China coast. Scattered references to Macau can easily be found in the index.

155 **The English in China: being an account of the intercourse and relations between England and China from the year 1600 to the year 1843 and a summary of later developments.**
    James Bromley Eames. London: Curzon; New York: Barnes & Noble, 1974. 585p. 2 maps.
Macau figures prominently in this study, especially during the periods when the English merchants were based in the city. Eames draws on the East India Company records and on some of the early English language literature to present his picture of the territory which was first published in 1909.

156 **The chronicles of the East India Company, trading to China 1635-1834.**
    Hosea Ballou Morse. Oxford: Clarendon, 1926. 4 vols. 5 maps.
References relating Macau to the East India Company can be found throughout the chronicles, from the description of the settlement of Macau in the mid-16th century (vol. I, p. 2) to the end of the fourth volume (vol. IV, p. 337).

A Macao narrative.
See item no. 119.

The Americans in Macau

157 **With the flowery banner: some comments on the Americans in Macao and south China.**
    José Maria Braga. Macau: N. T. Fernandes, 1940, 56p.
After an initial section on Portugal's rôle in the age of discovery, the focus shifts to the arrival of American ships at Macau in 1784. Braga relates incidents from the lives of Americans living in Macau up to the establishment of Hong Kong in 1842. In the later sections, Macau's contributions to American missionary and political activities in China during the 19th century are noted.

The Japanese in Macau

158 **Japanese Christians buried in the Jesuit college church of São Paulo at Macau.**
    Charles Ralph Boxer. *Monumenta Nipponica*, vol. 1 (1938) p. 265-69.
Lists the names of twenty-five lay Japanese Christians with detailed descriptions of their tomb sites. The last dated burial is from 1726.

159   **The Japanese in Macao in the XVIth and XVIIth centuries.**
Manuel Teixeira.   Macau: Imprensa Nacional, 1974. 22p.
Deals largely with the bones and other relics of Japanese martyrs and with the efforts
of Japanese workmen to build churches in Macau during the city's early history.
Subjects covered include: the building of São Paulo church (1602-03) and the relics of
Japanese martyrs kept in São Paulo; the rôle of Japanese in the so-called planned
Portuguese invasion of China (1606); the Christian martyrs of Nagasaki; the relics of
St. Francis Xavier in Macau; and the last attempt by the Portuguese to open Nagasaki.

Population

160 **Filhos da terra.** (Sons of the earth.)
Ana Maria de Sousa Marques da Silva Amaro. Macau: Instituto
Cultural, 1988, 123p. bibliog.
Relates the story of the Macaense people, ranging from blood types to cuisine.
Includes photographs of some famous Macaense, and of their crafts and customs.

161 **Macau e os seus habitantes: relações com Timor.** (Macau and its
residents: relations with Timor.)
Bento da França. Lisbon: Imprensa Nacional, 1897. 278p. 3 maps.
Contains a wide range of information about Macau from around the turn of the
century. Besides a description of the population, other topics such as geography,
history, administration, economic activities, customs and poems about Macau are also
covered. A separate section (p. 209-78) describes Portuguese Timor and its
relationship with Macau following their merger and creation as a separate province in
1844. An appendix (p. 279-82) describes the decree of 1896 which made Timor an
autonomous district.

162 **A história e os homens da primeira república democrática do Oriente:
biologia e sociologia de uma ilha cívica.** (A history of the people of the
first democratic republic of the Orient: the biology and sociology of a
civic island.)
Almerindo Lessa. Macau: Imprensa Nacional, 1974. 310p. map
This book first appeared in French as: *L'histoire et les hommes de la première
republique démocratique de l'Orient, anthropobiologie et anthroposociologie de
Macao* (Toulouse, France: Université de Toulouse, 1974). The Portuguese text
represents an expanded version of the original. Lessa discusses the spread of
Portuguese power in the tropics and gradually narrows down to a discussion of the
Portuguese on the China coast (in chapter three). Concerned primarily with the mixing
of peoples in the territory, including blood types and racial characteristics, Lessa

includes the results of a social survey undertaken in Macau during 1960 and concludes that Macau is a society with few racial prejudices.

163   **Macau, entroncamento de dois mundos.** (Macau: crossway of two worlds.)
      Mateus das Neves.   *Revista do Gabinete de Estudos Ultramarinos*, no. 9-10 (1953), p. 33-47.

Neves' main theme is that the Portuguese and Chinese communities have never intermingled in Macau. In his view the Macaense, while racially intermixed, are culturally Portuguese. Each culture considers itself superior to the other so that no blending takes place. The author, a priest, concludes that 'our Christian Latin civilization is undisputedly more superior'!

164   **Os Chins de Macau.** (The Chinese of Macau.)
      Manuel de Castro Sampaio.   Hong Kong: Typographia de Noronha, 1867. 144p. map.

Describes the Chinese in Macau in terms of their physical characteristics and their way of life. Food and drink, housing, law, religion, medicine, funerals, holidays, processions, superstitions, commerce and industry are all discussed. Sampaio finishes with a note about Macau Chinese emigration with particular reference to Peru and Cuba. Chinese population statistics for 1867 are presented by districts and emigration statistics are given for 1856-60.

165   **Interface of Chinese and Portuguese cultures.**
      Raymond A. Zepp.   In: *Macau: city of commerce and culture*. Edited by Rolf Dieter Cremer. Hong Kong: UEA Press, 1987, p. 125-36. bibliog.

Discusses the demographic changes in the proportions of Portuguese and Chinese, the amalgamation of cultures and the formation of the Macaense people. Zepp concludes that there has been relatively little mixing between Portuguese and Chinese cultures in Macau compared to the mixtures of Portuguese and native cultures in Africa and Southeast Asia.

O comércio de escravos em Macau: The so called Portuguese slave trade in Macao.
See item no. 134.

The demography of old Macao.
See item no. 128.

Os extremos conciliam-se (transculturação em Macau). (The extremes harmonize themselves: cultural interchange in Macau.)
See item no. 129.

Languages and Dialects

General

166 Estado actual do dialecto macaense. (The actual state of the Maquista dialect of Portuguese.)
Graciete Agostinho Nogueira Batalha.   *Revista Portuguesa de Filologia*, vol. 9 (1958), p. 177-213.
Seven years' residence in Macau and research into past studies of the Maquista dialect led the author to conclude that this local dialect of Portuguese was in rapid decline by the 1950s, mostly as a result of the influence of continental Portugal. Aspects of the old creole accent, mixing of gender usage and plural usage, combined with elements from Cantonese and Brazilian Portuguese characterize the Maquista dialect. The text, which includes a resumé in French, is also distributed as an off-print (Coimbra, Portugal: Revista Portuguesa de Filologia, 1959).

167 Língua de Macau: o que foi e o que é. (The language of Macau: what it was and what it is.)
Graciete Agostinho Noguiera Batalha.   Macau: Imprensa Nacional, 1974. 62p.
This amended and updated version of two journal articles published in 1958 begins with an introduction to the state of languages used in Macau in the 1950s and 1960s with emphasis on the Maquista dialect and the Macaense people. The introductory sections are followed by a more detailed discussion of the Maquista dialect with some vocabulary defined and linguistic characteristics described.

168 **Papiá cristam di Macau: epítome de gramática comparada e vocabulário.** (Papiá cristam di Macau: a compendium of comparative grammar and vocabulary.)
José dos Santos Ferreira. Macau: [n.p.], 1978. 107p.

A discussion of the linguistic structure of the Maquista dialect is followed by a glossary of vocabulary (p. 4-96) and a poem in the dialect.

169 **Centre for Portuguese language and culture.**
José Miguel Ribeiro Lume. In: *Macau: city of commerce and culture.* Edited by Rolf Dieter Cremer. Hong Kong. UEA Press, 1987, p. 115-23. map. bibliog.

A review of Portugal's presence in Asia and the spread of the Portuguese language, with some observations about the Maquista dialect. In conclusion, the author argues for the continuing rôle of Macau as a centre for the diffusion of Portuguese language and culture after 1999.

170 **A note on the origin of the name of Macao.**
Søren Egerod. *T'oung Pao,* vol. 47 (1959), p. 63-66. bibliog.

Reviews possible derivations of the Portuguese name of Macau. Egerod believes the Portuguese name 'Macau' comes from the Cantonese *Má-kóng* (Standard Chinese, *Mǎgâng*) or 'Mother barbour', rather than from some of the other conventional attributions such as *Á-má-ou* (Ámā aò) or 'Bay of the Goddess Ama' or Má Kông (Mǎ Gōng) or 'Temple of Ama'.

171 **Two synchronic cross-sections in the Portuguese dialect of Macao.**
Robert Wallace Thompson. *Orbis: Bulletin International de Documentation Linguistique,* vol. 8, no. 1 (June 1959), p. 29-53.

Words in the Maquista dialect transliterated for a glossary to the Chinese geography of 1751, *Aòmén Jìlüè* (q.v.), are compared with those used in the modern version of the dialect as spoken amongst immigrants in Hong Kong. Most of the article (p. 37-53) is a comparative glossary of terms.

172 **Chinese dialects in Macau.**
Woon, Wee Lee. In: *Macau: city of commerce and culture.* Edited by Rolf Dieter Cremer. Hong Kong: UEA Press, 1987, p. 103-13. 2. maps. bibliog.

A general discussion of Chinese languages is followed by a section on Cantonese or Yuè. The relation of Macau Cantonese to the Zhongshan dialect and standard Cantonese of Guangzhou is considered. Gradually, the local Zhongshan dialect has become dominated by Guangzhou Cantonese. Mention is made of the southern Mín language of Fujian and the Wú language of the Shanghai area which are also spoken by a minority of Macau's Chinese. For business and general communication all Chinese in Macau learn to speak Guangzhou Cantonese.

Dictionaries and grammars

173 **Glossário do dialecto macaense: notas linguísticas, etnográficas e folclóricas.** (A glossary of the Maquista dialect: linguistic, ethnographic and folkloric notes.)
Graciete Agostinho Nogueira Batalha. Macau: Instituto Cultural, 1988. 336p. bibliog.

Lists words in the Maquista dialect in alphabetical order with an explanation in Standard Portuguese. The words are drawn from a range of texts and examples of usage are supplied. The glossary, which includes a resumé in French, was previously published as a reprint from the *Revista Portuguesa de Filologia (Faculdade de Letras da Universidade de Coimbra)*, 1977. 338p. bibliog. This version has been updated by the *Suplemento ao glossário do dialecto macaense* (q.v.).

174 **Suplemento ao glossário do dialecto macaense: novas notas linguísticas, etnográficas e folclóricas.** (Supplement to the glossary of the Maquista dialect: new linguistic, ethnographic and folkloric notes.) Graciete Agostinho Noguiera Batalha. macau: Instituto Cultural. 1988. 80p. bibliog.

An updated version of the *Glossário do dialecto macaense* (q.v.) based on discoveries made by the author between 1977 and 1987. Includes thirty-seven illustrations.

175 **Glossário luso-asiático.** (A Luso-Asiatic glossary.)
Sebastião Rodolpho Dalgado. Coimbra, Portugal: Imprensa da Universidade, 1919-21. 2 vols. bibliog.

A glossary of words which have entered the Portuguese language from various Asian languages. Although most of the vocabulary included in the 1,054 pages come from the Indian subcontinent, Chinese words, many of which entered Portuguese via Macau, are also included.

176 **Dicionário chinês-português.** (A Chinese-Portuguese dictionary.)
Governo de Macau. Macau: Imprensa Nacional, 1962. 921p.

The largest Chinese-Portuguese dictionary published in this century, this work was undertaken by a Macau committee of three; using Cantonese-English, Chinese-French, and Standard Chinese-Cantonese dictionaries as the basis of the project. The entries are arranged alphabetically and according to Portuguese romanization of Cantonese. As such, the dictionary is quite helpful for the conversion of Cantonese proper names into Portuguese.

177 **Dicionário português-chinês.** (New standard Portuguese-Chinese dictionary.)
Governo de Macau. Macau: Imprensa Nacional, [1971]. 1864p.

The most detailed Portuguese-Chinese dictionary available, this book was pirated in Taipei, China as *The new standard Portuguese-Chinese dictionary* by the Shin Lou Book Company in 1983.

178 **Método de português para uso das escolas chinesas.** (Method of
Portuguese language for use in the Chinese schools.)
Edited by António André Ngan. Macau: Imprensa Nacional, 1982-
1987. 6 vols.

Portuguese language textbook for Cantonese speaking students, arranged in three
volumes with two parts each. Subjects concerned with Christianity and with Macau are
emphasized.

Religion

179 **Macau, mãe das missões no Extremo Oriente.** (Macau, mother of the
missions of East Asia.)
Eusébio Arnáiz, translated from the Spanish by Artur Augusto
Neves.   Macau: Tipografia Salesiana, 1957. 182p. 2 maps. bibliog.

Originally published in the Boletim Eclesiástico , this volume presents, in a positive
light, the efforts of the Macau-based missions to convert China and Japan to
Catholicism. Individual chapters discuss the work of the various religious orders based
in Macau.

180 **Aux portes de la Chine: les missionaries du seizième siècle 1514-1588.**
(At the gates of China: the missionaries of the 16th century 1514-1588.)
Henri Bernard.   Tientsin, China: Hautes Études, 1933. 283p.

Divides the study period into two, for the years 1514-81, when the Portuguese and
Spanish priests failed to penetrate mainland China, and the period 1581-89, when a
group of Italian priests disassociated themselves as much as possible from the
foreigners of Macau and suceeded in getting into China. Chapter six (p. 87-102) is a
review of early Portuguese settlement and religious activities in Macau. The unique
element in this book is its emphasis on the conflict between Iberian and Italian
missionaries, whereas other authors have emphasized hostilities between Portuguese
and Spanish or Portuguese and French missionary efforts operating in and out of
Macau.

181 **Boletim Eclesial.** (Ecclesiastical Bulletin.)
Macau: Câmera Eclesiástica da Diocese de Macau, 1980-. monthly.

This is the official organ of the Diocese of Macau and is divided into four parts with
each issue roughly seventy pages long. The first part includes official religious
statements, many of them relevant to Macau. The second part, entitled 'Religious
Sciences', focuses on bible or spiritual studies. The third part is called 'Human
Sciences' and frequently contains articles on religious problems in Macau, often of a

historical nature. The final section, 'For the Diocese of Macau' contains notes on charitable societies in Macau, and notices of lectures. This bulletin is a continuation of the *Boletim Eclesiástico da Diocese de Macau* which began in 1904.

182   **A igreja de S. Domingos e os Dominicanos em Macau.** (The church of São Domingos and the Dominicans in Macau.)
José Maria Braga.   Macau: Orfanato de Imaculada Conceição, 1939. 46p.

Relates the story of the Dominican order in Macau beginning with the founding of a church in the mid-16th century and the problems which the order faced because of its patronage by Spain. Information is given on Dominican missionary activities in China and there is considerable detail on the rôle the São Domingos church has played in the history of Macau. Festivals connected with the church are also cited.

183   **Diocesan Echo.**
Hong Kong: Diocesan Literature Committee, 1981-[1984] monthly.

A newsletter for the Anglican Church community, which mostly concerns Hong Kong, although it is published for the Diocese of Hong Kong and Macau.

184   **Tomb-stones in the English cemeteries at Macao.**
José Maria Braga.   Macau: Publicity Office Macao Economic Services Department, 1940. 59p.

Until 1821, there was no public cemetery in Macau. Catholics were buried in parish churchyards, British East India Company Protestants were buried on the Company grounds while others were buried outside the city walls. In 1821, a Protestant cemetery was established which was soon filled so that a new Protestant cemetery had to be founded in 1856. Short histories of these cemeteries accompany lists of the tombstone engravings found therein with a final list of entries from the 'register of burials' for which no gravestones have been found.

185   **Rodrigues the interpreter: an early Jesuit in Japan and China.**
Michael Cooper.   New York; Tokyo: Weatherhill, 1974. 357p. bibliog.

A narrative biography of Father João Rodrigues (ca. 1561-1633) who spent fifty-six years in Japan, Macau and China as a Jesuit missionary. Rodrigues is best known for his influence on Toyotomi Hideyoshi and Tokugawa Ieyasu and for his Japanese grammar and history of the Church in Japan. In 1610, he was exiled to Macau and was based there until his death in 1633. Macau figures throughout this book but there are two major discussions of the territory: a description of the city in 1610 (p. 269-76) and a chapter on Rodrigues' work in Macau entitled 'Business in Macao' (p. 313-30).

186   **The wise man from the West.**
Vincent Cronin.   London: Rupert Hart-Davis, 1955. 300p. 2 maps, bibliog.

Presents a history of the life of Matteo Ricci. Macau figures throughout as one of the backdrops in this dramatized history.

Religion

187 **A expansão da fé no Extremo Oriente (subsidios para a história colonial).** (The expansion of the faith in the Far East: aids for a colonial history.
António Lourenço Farinha.   Lisbon: Agência Geral das Colónias, 1946, 3 vols.
Volume three of this history contains a chapter on the Diocese of Macau from its beginnings in the 16th century up to 1939 (p. 143-205). The chapter includes a section on the Portuguese padroado as well as a list of the Diocese's bishops.

188 **Anuário católico do ultramar português: Annuaire catholique de l'outre-mer portugais.** (The Catholic yearbook of Portuguese overseas territories.)
Compiled by Albano Mendes Pedro.   Lisbon: Junta de Investigações do Ultramar, Centro de Estudos Missionários, 1965. 2nd ed. 701p.
The section on Macau (p. 612-45) lists all the churches and their staff for Macau, Singapore and Malacca, and includes the missions in Guangdong province, China, which were under Macau's jurisdiction until 1949.

189 **Missões católicas portuguesas: documentário fotográfico: Missions catholiques de l'outre-mer portugais: documentaire photographique.**
(The Portuguese Catholic missions: a photographic documentary.)
Compiled and introduced by Albano Mendes Pedro.   Lisbon: Junta de Investigações do Ultramar, Centro de Estudos Históricos Ultramarinos, 1964. 159p. 20 maps.
Macau is covered on p. 149-53 of this bilingual photographic album which features all the bishops and the major churches in Portugal's former overseas empire. Basic statistics and a map are included.

190 **O padroado portuguez na China.** (The Portuguese padroado in China.)
A. Marques Pereira.   Lisbon: J. G. de Sousa Neves, 1873. 36p.
A collection of letters published in Lisbon newspapers accompanied by comments on the planned restriction of the Portuguese padroado which had given the Bishop of Macau control over Catholic missions in East Asia. From 1690, Macau's control was restricted to Guangdong and Guangxi. After 1860, the Diocese of Macau was further reduced to Guangdong only with Hong Kong excluded. The author discusses the attempt by the Holy See to restrict the Bishop of Macau's diocese to the city of Macau and to give control of missionary work in Guangdong to a French group. Although opposed to this, Marques Pereira prints the responses of the other side in this newspaper debate alongside his own letters to the editors.

191 **Curso de missionologia.** (A course in missionology).
António da Silva Rego.   Lisbon: Agência Geral do Ultramar, 1956. 589p. 13 maps.
Presents a history of Portuguese missionary work in various countries. Macau is discussed as a port of entry for missionaries to China (p. 405-31) and to Japan (p. 433-79).

46

192　**Les missions portugaises (aperçu général).** (The Portuguese missions: a general overview.
António da Silva Rego.　Lisbon: Agência Geral do Ultramar, 1958. 71p.
This overview of the Portuguese mission movement contains a discussion of Macau's part in the mission to China (p. 24-27). There is also a general survey of the Diocese of Macau in 1958 (p. 50-51).

193　**China in the sixteenth century: the journals of Matthew Ricci: 1583-1610.**
Matteo Ricci, Nicola Trigault, translated from the Latin by Louis J. Gallagher.　New York: Random House, 1953. 594p.
The diary of Matteo Ricci, one of the most famous missionaries to China, translated from Italian to Latin and amended by Nicola Trigault in 1615. Ricci spent the year of 1582-83 in Macau preparing for his mission work and some of the city's Jesuit mission efforts are described in this book.

194　**As Canossianas na Diocese de Macau: 1 centenário (1874-1974).** (The Canossians in the Diocese of Macau: the first century (1874-1974).)
Manuel Teixeira.　Macau: Tipografia da Missão do Padroado, 1974. 336p.
Presents the complete history of the Canossian order's charitable activities in Macau with separate sections on Timor, Singapore and Malacca.

195　**The church in Macau.**
Manuel Teixeira.　In: *Macau: city of commerce and culture*. Edited by Rolf Dieter Cremer. Hong Kong: UEA Press, 1987, p. 39-49. bibliog.
A brief history of the Catholic Church's activities in Macau over the centuries with emphasis on missionary work and church construction. British Protestant mission activities in Macau are also mentioned.

196　**The fourth centenary of Jesuits at Macao.**
Manuel Teixeira.　Macau: Salesian School of Printers, 1964, 60p.
Relates the history of the Jesuits in Macau, including a description of their buildings, a list of major events related to the order from 1564 to 1964, and some stories of early Jesuit martyrs. A final section gives information about individual Portuguese and Chinese Jesuits who were involved in mission work in Macau and China.

197　**Macau e a sua diocese.** (Macau and its diocese.)
Manuel Teixeira.　Macau, Lisbon: [n.p.], 1940-82. 16 vols.
This is the ultimate series for anyone interested in details of religious activity in Macau. Volumes relevant to Macau are: volume one, *Macau e as suas ilhas.* (Macau and its islands.) (Macau: Escola Tipografica Salesiana, 1940. 250p. 3 maps), a general introductory volume which contains an account of Macau's origins, history and historic buildings; volume two, *Bispos e governadores do bispado de Macau.* (Bishops and governors of the bishopric of Macau.) (Macau: Imprensa Nacional, 1940. 538p.), which contains chapters about each bishop; volume three, *As ordens e congregações religiosas*

Religion

em Macau. (Religious orders and congregations in Macau.) (Macau: Tipografia Soi Sang, 1956-1961. 820p.), which provides details about the diocese which then included Hainan, Timor and Malacca as well as information about the various religious orders in the diocese; volume seven, *Padres da diocese de Macau*. (Priests of the diocese of Macau.) (Macau: Tipografia da Missão do Padroado, 1967. 651p.), which provides a directory of teachers and brothers from the 16th to the 20th centuries as well as notes on martyrs in Japan, China, Korea and Tonkin; volume eight, *Padres da diocese de Macau*. (Priests of the diocese of Macau.) (Macau; Tipografia da Missão do Padroado, 1972); volume nine, *O culto de Maria em Macau*. (The cult of the Virgin Mary in Macau.) (Macau: Tipografia da Missão do Padroado, 1969. 468p.), which describes churches, festivals, fortresses and aspects of religious life connected with the blessed Virgin; volume eleven, *As confrarias em Macau*. (The fraternal orders in Macau.) (Macau: Tipografia da Missão do Padroado, 1975); volume twelve, *Bispos, missionários, igrejas e escolas*. (Bishops, missionaries, churches and schools.) (Macau: Tipografia da Missádo do Padroado, 1976. 524p.), which includes information on social welfare organizations of the church; and volume fifteen, *Relações comerciais de Macau com o Vietnam*. (Macau's commercial relations with Vietnam.) (Macau: Imprensa Nacional, 1977. 295p.), which discusses the period prior to 1874 drawing on considerable documentation.

198 **A precious treasure in Coloane.**

Manuel Teixeira. Macau: Department of Tourism and Information, 1980. 2nd ed. 28p.

Texeira relates the story of the death of St. Francis Xavier in 1552 and tells how one bone from the saint's arm ended up in São Francisco Xavier Church in Coloane. Also described are the relics of Japanese and Vietnamese martyrs stored in the church. The story of the most famous of the Vietnamese martyrs, known as André, is told in detail.

199 **The Protestant cemeteries of Macau.**

Manuel Teixeira. Macau: Direcção dos Serviços de Turismo, 1984. 124p. 3 maps.

Begins with a brief history of the founding of the old and new Protestant cemeteries. Lists of tombstone inscriptions are accompanied by notes on some of the famous people buried in the old cemetery including Robert Morrison, Sir Anders Ljungstedt and George Chinnery.

An architectural survey of the Jesuit seminary church of St. Paul's, Macao.
See item no. 294.

The church of St. Paul in Macau.
See item no. 299.

Contribution to an historical sketch of the Portuguese settlements in China, principally of Macao, and of the Portuguese envoys & ambassadors to China, of the Roman Catholic mission in China and of the Papal legates to China.
See item no. 125.

The convent and church of St. Dominic at Macao.
See item no. 295.

An historical sketch of the Portuguese settlements in China; and of the Roman Catholic Church and missions in China.
See item no. 126.

The parish church of St. Lawrence at Macao.
See item no. 296.

Japanese Christians buried in the Jesuit college church of São Paulo at Macau.
See item no. 158.

The Japanese in Macao in the XVIth and XVIIth centuries.
See item no. 159.

L'orfanotrofio di Macau e la missione dell'Heung-shan in Cina. (The orphanage of Macau and the mission at Xiangshan in China.)
See item no. 205.

Social Conditions

Social problems

200 **Cities of sin.**
Hendrik de Leeuw. London: Neville Spearman, 1953. 4th ed. 231p.
First published in 1934, this story of woman and vice covers the cities of Yokohama, Hong Kong, Shanghai, Macau (p. 136-80), Port Said and Singapore. De Leeuw discusses the cases of several unfortunate women in Macau and the loopholes in the territory's prostitution laws. There is a racist as well as a sensual tone to the writing.

201 **La colonie de Macao et la question du trafic de l'opium.** (The colony of Macau and the question of the opium traffic.)
J. Caeiro da Matta. Lisbon: Imprensa Portugal-Brasil, 1940. 95p.
The author defends Portugal's opium policies in Macau. An accusation was put forward by the US delegate to the League of Nations Permanent Central Committee for Opium that more opium was imported to Macau than was normally used in the colony through the government's opium monopoly. The excess was thought to be entering the international market. Included are statements made by the Portuguese to the Committee during August 1938 and May 1940 as well as a report on an opium survey undertaken by the Portuguese government in Macau during the mid-1930s.

Social services, health and welfare

202 **Saúde 85: Health '85.**
Edited by Direcção dos Serviços de Saúde de Macau. Macau: Gabinete de Comunicação Social do Governo de Macau, 1985. 38p. 2 maps.
This pamphlet presents a general overview of Macau's geography and demography followed by a discussion of plans for improving the territory's health services during

Social Conditions. Social services, health and welfare

1986. A similar pamphlet was written for 1984 and subsequent pamphlets may be published. The text, which is trilingual, includes forty-three tables with geographical, demographic, and economic data as well as statistics strictly related to health. The English version contains many textual errors.

203   **A sanidade de Macau (traços de hygiene urbana e social).** (Health conditions in Macau: aspects of urban and social hygiene.)
Antonio do Nascimento Leitão.   Macau: Imprensa Nacional. 1909. 55p.

This paper, given at the Macau Military Club, presents a grim picture of health conditions and vice in Macau around the turn of the century. In conclusion, the author argues that improvement hinges on plans to dredge the Porto Interior, since an improved harbour would facilitate arrival of medical goods, and, more importantly, lead to prosperity.

204   **Housing in Macau.**
Li, Shu-fan, Poon, Sheung-tak, Yeung, Chee-on. *Annals of the Geographical, Geological and Archeological Society, Hong Kong University*, no. 1 (1972), p. 8-16. map. bibliog.

The authors note that Macau faced a severe housing problem in the early 1970s with a shortage of nearly 45,000 units. They provide a description of squatter conditions and an account of Macau's public housing programme.

205   **L'orfanotrofio di Macau e la missione dell'Heung-shan in Cina.** (The orphanage of Macau and the mission at Xiangshan in China.)
Edited by the Missioni Salesiane.   Torino, Italy: Società Editrice Internazionale, 1925. 81p.

The first section (p. 3-17) describes the Salesian orphanage in Macau from its founding in 1906 to 1923. The buildings and cultural activities are considered, the text is well illustrated with photographs, and tables are provided for annual numbers of students, baptisms, community size and contributions to the Mission.

206   **O Centro de Recuperação Social da Ilha da Taipa em Macau.** (The Social Rehabilitation Centre on the Island of Taipa, Macau.)
Sigismundo Revés, Alberto Cotta Guerra.   Lisbon: Agência Geral do Ultramar, 1962. 45p.

Presents an illustrated history of the Centre and its antecedents, from the drug rehabilitation programmes which began in 1946 to the founding of the Centre in 1960. A detailed description of the Centre's operation in 1961-62 is also provided.

207   **Macao.**
Harry Redl.   Hong Kong: Dragonfly, 1963. 100p. 2 maps.

An album of photographs with accompanying text presenting a positive view of the Portuguese Macau government and scorning the policies of the People's Republic of China. The pictures give a good account of life in Macau during the early 1960s. Some very interesting shots of the drug rehabilitation efforts on Taipa are included.

Social Conditions. Social services, health and welfare

208 **Macau e a assistência (panorama médico-social).** (Macau and welfare: a socio-medical viewpoint.)
José Caetano Soares. Lisbon: Agência Geral das Colónias, 1950. 539p.

Traces all aspects of welfare in Macau from their beginnings under Bishop D. Belchior Carneiro in the second half of the 16th century down to 1950. Some mission-related welfare undertaken in China is also discussed.

209 **A medicina em Macau.** (Medicine in Macau.)
Manuel Teixeira. Macau: Imprensa Nacional, 1975-76. 4 vols.

Volume one, *Assistência médica em Macau*, relates the history of all hospitals in the territory. Volume two, *A nosologia em Macau*, discusses Chinese medicine and general sanitation in the territory as well as leprosy, smallpox, influenza, malaria, tuberculosis, venereal disease, mental illness, drug addiction, and other diseases. Volumes three and four, *Os médicos em Macau*, list all the doctors practising Western medicine in Macau between the 16th and 19th centuries and during the 20th century with additional information about the doctors' careers.

210 **Os médicos em Macau.** (Doctors in Macau.)
Manuel Teixeira. Macau: Centro de Informação e Turismo, Imprensa Nacional, 1967. 104p.

Originally published in the *Boletim do Instituto Luís de Camões*, vol. 2, no. 1 (October 1967), this book presents short sketches from the lives of doctors who practised in Macau. It is divided into three sections, for the 17th century, the 18th century and the 19th century.

Politics

General administration

211 **Guia prático das eleições para assembleia legislativa de Macau.** (A practical guide to the elections for the legislative assembly of Macau.) [Governo de Macau].   Macau: [n.p.], [1976]. [11p.]
Provides an illustrated guide on how to vote with other fine points on election procedures.

212 **Estatuto político-administrativo da Província de Macau.** (The political administrative statute of the Province of Macau.)
Ministério do Ultramar.   Lisbon: Agência Geral do Ultramar, 1963. 31p.
Published in response to a government order that all statutes for Portuguese overseas provinces should be revised, this pamphlet describes the organs of government for Macau during the leadership of Dr. António de Oliveira Salazar in Portugal (1932-68). Included are sections on the functions of the Governor, the legislative council, the government council, public service, local government, and financial bodies.

213 **Estatuto político-administrativo da Província de Macau.** (The political administrative statute of the Province of Macau.)
Governo de Portugal.   Lisbon: Agência Geral do Ultramar, 1972. 45p.
Describes the way in which the administration of Macau was intended to function from 1972 to 1974.

214 **De Macau.** (On Macau.)
Edited by the União Nacional de Macau. Macau: Tipografia do
Orfanato Salesiano, 1940. 137p.

Presents the Macau government's picture of plans for and local accomplishments of
Dr. Salazar's *Estado Novo* in 1937-38. Includes statements and photographs relating to
education, the military and the development of postal and telegraphic communications.
The history of the territory is covered both before and after the rise of Salazar to
power in Portugal, and colonial legislation, economy and finance are also discussed.
Other subjects discussed in this document are Catholic missions, ports, public health,
aviation, the conflict between family and state in Macau and China, and judicial
reforms.

215 **Eanes e as mistérios de Macau.** (President Eanes and the mysteries of
Macau.)
Rola da Silva. Lisbon: Vozes da Tribo, 1985. 183p.

A criticism of political corruption in Macau during the Governorship of Vasco Almeida
e Costa by a journalist who lived in Macau at the time and wrote for the newspaper,
Tribuna de Macau.

216 **Macau coordenadas de política cultural.** (Macau: politico-cultural co-
ordinates.)
Macau: Instituto Cultural, 1986. 82p.

Two lectures on cultural policy in Macau, one by the Governor and the other by the
president of the Instituto Cultural de Macau, are accompanied by copies of statutes
covering the period of 1982-86. The statutes refer, among other things, to the
preservation of architecture on Macau and to the establishment of the Instituto
Cultural de Macau and the Centro Cultural Sir Robert Ho Tung.

Administração: Hâng Chêng (Xíng Zhèng).
See item no. 355.

Os militares em Macau. (The military in Macau.)
See item no. 144.

Constitution and legal system

217 **The constitution and legal system.**
Rui António Craveiro Afonso, Francisco Gonçalves Pereira. In:
Macau: city of commerce and culture. Edited by Rolf Dieter Cremer.
Hong Kong: UEA Press, 1987, p. 185-98. bibliog.

A revised and abridged edition of 'The political statutes and government institutions of
Macao' published in the *Hong Kong Law Journal* (q.v.), this article describes the
constitution of Macau and the distribution of power amongst the three law-making
authorities in the territory. Power in Macau is divided between the branches of the

Portuguese government, the Macau Legislative Assembly (Assembleia Legislativa), and the Governor, as well as the administrative divisions of government. The authors elucidate the local judical system and its relation to the Portuguese legal system, noting the transition to more bilingual laws and Chinese-style legal practices.

218 **The political status and government institutions of Macao.**
Rui António Craveiro Afonso, Francisco Gonçalves Pereira. *Hong Kong Law Journal*, no. 16 (1986). p. 28-57.
This is an earlier version of the article 'The constitution and legal system' (q.v.) which appeared in *Macau: city of commerce and culture*. The authors include a section on the territory's legal system until the 19th century, which was not incorporated in the later article. Much of the discussion focuses on the Portuguese payment of ground rent to the Chinese which began in 1573.

219 **Macao: legal fiction and gunboat diplomacy.**
Anthony R. Dicks. In: *Leadership on the China coast*. Edited by Göran Aijmer London; Malmö, Sweden: Curzon, 1984, p. 90-128. (Scandinavian Institute of Asian Studies, Studies on Asian Topics, no. 8).
Despite the date of this publication, this article appears to have been written in the late 1960s. Dicks describes in detail the events of the eight months during 1966-67 when rioting occurred in Macau and Portuguese authority was seriously undermined. The political and legal implications of these events are discussed.

220 **The international status of Macao before 1887.**
George W. Keeton. *Chinese Social and Political Science Review*, vol. 11, no. 3 (July 1927), p. 404-13.
Sets out in concise terms the relationship of legal jurisdiction between China, Portugal, and Britain before the Protocol of Lisbon in 1887 which gave Portugal right of perpetual occupation of Macau. The early history section suffers from the author's sole reliance on English language sources. However, the strength of the article is that it does show the political rôle played by Britain in early Macau.

221 **Macau.**
Peter Wesley-Smith. *Constitutions of dependencies and special sovereignties*. Edited by Albert P. Blaustein, Phyllis M. Blaustein. Dobbs Ferry, New York: Oceana, 1987. 93p. bibliog.
Contains English, Portuguese and Chinese versions of the constitution (Estatuto Orgânico de Macau) enacted 10 February 1976 in seventy-six articles. There is also a copy of the joint declaration of 1987 on the question of Macao.

Boletim Oficial. (The Official Bulletin.)
See item no. 361.

Cities of sin.
See item no. 200.

Macau in Sino-Portuguese relations: the pre-1974 view

222 **A política europeia no Extremo Oriente no século XIX e as nossas relações diplomáticas com a China.** (European politics in the Far East in the 19th century and our diplomatic relations with China.)
Eduardo Brazão. Oporto, Portugal: Livraria Civilização, 1938. 87p.
The diplomatic history of Macau in Sino-Portuguese relations is discussed from the Portuguese viewpoint (p. 30-44). Two documents are appended: one is a short treatise on political relations between China and the West, written in 1859, and the other an account of an embassy to the Chinese emperor, dated 1753.

223 **Macau: perspectiva histórica.** (Macau: an historical perspective.)
António da Silva Rego. Lisbon: Junta de Investigações do Ultramar, 1966. 14p.
The author sees Macau's history as unique amongst Portugal's colonies because of the territory's weak position *vis à vis* China. Two events are described to illustrate the special relationship between Portugal and China: the pressure exerted by the Chinese against the British presence in Macau during 1808 and the restoration of Portugal's former privileges after providing aid to fight pirates in 1810. In conclusion, Silva Rego adopts the Chinese view of the Portuguese presence in Macau as a sovereignty of service, rather than the Portuguese view of their rôle as a sovereignty of domination. To Silva Rego, the service aspect is still present and visible in the aid given to Chinese refugees and to Chinese nationals at the Drug Addiction Centre. This article was first published in *Províncias portuguesas do Oriente* (Universade Technica de Lisboa, 1966-67).

224 **Conjuntura de Macau.**
António Lopes dos Santos. Lisbon: Junta de Investigações do Ultramar, 1966. 42p.
First published in *Provincias portuguesas do Oriente* (Universidade Technica de Lisboa, 1966-67), this text is divided into three main parts. A brief section on Macau's past is followed by a detailed discussion of geographical, social and economic trends accompanied by fifteen graphs showing trends from 1955 to 1965. Hospital quality and levels of education are seen as particularly high for a Portuguese overseas province. A third section discusses the political future of Macau. Portugal's continued presence in Macau is seen as dependent on the country's continued neutral and non-belligerent status. The author, a military man, argues for three policies to improve Portugal's position: an increase in cultural studies, in particular the education of the Chinese and others, with the Instituto Luís de Camões as the main focus; the maintenance of open scrutiny by international organizations of Portugal's activities in Macau, and the creation of economic promotional organizations in Macau to enhance Portuguese and East Asian trade.

Macau in Sino-Portuguese relations: the return of Macau to China

225 **Settlement of the Macao issue: distinctive features of Beijing's negotiating behavior.**
Jaw-ling Joanne Chang. *Case Western Reserve Journal of International Law*, vol. 20, no. 1 (Winter 1988), p. 253-78. Reprinted Baltimore, Maryland: University of Maryland School of Law, 1988. 37p. (Occasional Papers/Reprints Series in Contemporary Asian Studies, no. 87).

After providing a brief historical background, Chang discusses the negotiations over Macau's return to China and considers Beijing's negotiating tactics. She concludes that for Beijing the Macau negotiations were different from those of Hong Kong and that Chinese tactics included insisting on Beijing as the negotiating site, setting a deadline for resolution of the issue, and reopening already resolved issues as a post-negotiation manoeuvre.

226 **A model for Macau?**
Rolf Dieter Cremer. *Asian Affairs, An American Review*, (Winter 1987), p. 41-45.

Although the author's predictions for Macau's political future are not completely accurate, the article provides a concise description of Macau's political system around 1985 and suggests areas where transition to Chinese rule will not prove too difficult.

227 **Declaração conjunta Sino-Portuguesa sobre a questão de Macau.** (The Sino-Portuguese joint declaration on the question of Macau.)
The People's Republic of China, the Republic of Portugal. Beijing: Waiwen Chubanshe, 1987. 83p.

Although the title is only given in Chinese and Portuguese, the appendix contains a complete translation of the declaration into English (p. 57-83). This document represents the basis for the future of the territory after 20 December 1999.

Centre for Portuguese language and culture.
See item no. 169.

Economy

General

228 **China, Japan and the Asian NICs, Hong Kong and Macau, Singapore, South Korea, Taiwan, economic structure and analysis.**
London: Economist Intelligence Unit, 1988. 194p. 7 maps.
The section on Macau (p. 111-17) gives a brief political introduction followed by details on employment, various sectors of the economy, finance, foreign trade, and foreign debt. The data used in this book is drawn from the years 1981 to 1986.

229 **Country profile: Hong Kong, Macau.**
London: Economist Intelligence Unit, 1986-. annual. maps. bibliog.
Presents a more detailed profile than that found in the *Country Report: Hong Kong, Macau* (q.v.). Although some historical, political and social information is given, the major emphasis is on the economy.

230 **Country Report: Hong Kong, Macau.**
London: Economist Intelligence Unit, 1986-. quarterly.
Reports on economic and political events which have occurred in Macau. This is a good source for up-to-date economic information.

231 **Macau's modern economy.**
Renato Feitor. In: *Macau: city of commerce and culture.* Edited by Rolf Dieter Cremer. Hong Kong: UEA Press, 1987, p. 139-53.
Divides recent economic development in Macau into two periods: the 1970s with rapid growth and the 1980s with increased diversification and modernization. The future for Macau's economy is uncertain due to foreign competition from less developed countries and protectionism in the developed countries. Feitor argues for greater government efforts to improve Macau's infrastructure and image. The Macau-Zhuhai connection is also discussed.

Economy. General

232 Caracterização da economia de Macau. (The make-up of Macau's economy.)
Edited by Gabinete de Comunicação Social. Macau: Governo de Macau, [1986]. 186p.

Compiled by several branches of the Macau government and elucidated by numerous tables, the book presents an analysis of Macau's economy and the territory's political and legal system in 1985. Trends in major industries such as textiles and clothing, toys and sporting goods, and artificial flowers are discussed in detail. The sections on external commerce include specific discussions of relations with Hong Kong, the People's Republic of China, the EEC, the USA, and Portugal.

233 Relatório de execução do plano de investimentos (1983-1984): Investment plan execution report (1983-1984).
Edited by Governo de Macau. Macau: The Author, [1985], 82p.

A well-illustrated publication which gives separate reports of budget expenditures for 1983 and 1984 in Portuguese, Chinese, and English. Eighty-seven per cent of total budget expenditure in 1984 was absorbed by the categories of 'basic infrastructure', 'education, culture, and sports', 'housing', and 'modernization of public administration'. Smaller amounts were spent, in descending order, on 'transport and communications', 'health', 'physical (land-use) planning', 'tourism', 'basic studies and research', and 'the environment'.

234 Macau's economic role in the West River delta.
John T. Kamm. In: Macau: city of commerce and culture. Edited by Rolf Dieter Cremer. Hong Kong: UEA Press, 1987, p. 165-83. map. bibliog.

After considerable dicussion of economic activity in the western Pearl River delta, Macau's economic relations with China and the rôle of the People's Republic in Macau are both described. It is Kamm's belief that Macau can play a major rôle as an entrepôt for the western side of the Pearl River delta if given strong political support by China and Portugal.

235 Economy of Macau.
Compiled by Wong Hon-Keung, translated by Hunang Wei-Wen. Macau: Jornal Va Kio, 1988. 539p.

This English translation of Ou Mun kêng châi nin kám (q.v.) provides encyclopaedic coverage of various industries followed by discussion: import and export trade; building and the property market; tourism;agriculture and fishing; commerce; communciation; water and electricity; the financial system and family finance. Included are many colour plates showing landscape and factory conditions in Macau as well as aerial photographs.

Exportação especial por países: Special export by countries.
See item no. 247.

Macau: a mais antiga colónia europeia no Extremo-Oriente. (Macau: the oldest European colony in East Asia.)
See item no. 9.

59

Linhas de acção governativa, plano de investimentos: análise de situação económica e financeira do território. (Lines of government action, investment plan: an analysis of the economic and financial situation of the territory.)
See item no. 54.

Ou Mun kêng châi nin kám. (Aòmén jīngjì niánjiàn). (Almanac of Macau's economy 1984-1986).
See item no. 367.

Síntese da evolução de alguns indicadores sócio-económicos 1981-1985. (A synthesis of the evolution of several socio-economic indicators 1981-1985.)
See item no. 246.

Finance and banking

236 **Portugals Macau Chinas tor zur Welt: eine politische und wirtschaftliche Analyse für investoren und kaufleute ; Territory of Macau Chinas [sic] gate to the West: a political and economic analysis for investors and business-men [sic].**
Roland Braun, Thomas Jetter.   Heidelberg, GFR: Klemmerberg, 1985. 71p. map.
A general introduction is followed by a detailed description of the banking sector of Macau up to around 1983. Other economic information and details of the territory's infrastructure are also supplied. The pamphlet is written in German with a complete English translation (p. 37-71).

237 **Currency of Macau.**
Ma Tak-wo.   Hong Kong: Urban Council, 1987. 83p.
This history of bank notes, pangtang (cash deposit certificates) and coins of the territory is illustrated in colour. A summary of events in the development of Macau's currency is also provided. The text is in Chinese and English.

The Hongkong and Shanghai Banking Corporation business profile series: Macau.
See item no. 10.

Industry, Agriculture and Transport

Industry

238 **Macau e a sua primeira exposição industrial e feira: Macao and its first industrial and commercial fair 1926.**
João Carlos Alves, João Barbosa Pires.   Macau: Direcção das Obras dos Portos. 1926. 81p. 4 maps.
A bilingual pamphlet in Portuguese and English which provides an introduction to Macau followed by details of the organization and layout of the territory's first industrial and commercial fair held in November and December 1926. The authors include a discussion of products displayed at the fair, while a final section outlines plans for the expansion of Macau's ports.

239 **Agreement between the European Economic Community and Macao on trade in textile products, Brussels, 14 January 1877.**
European Economic Community.   London: HMSO, 1978. 15p.
Provides the text of the agreement on limitations of Macau's textile imports to the EEC from 1975 to 1977.

Inquérito industrial 1980. (Industrial inquiry 1980.)
See item no. 248.

Agriculture

240 **Agro-pecuária em Macau: aspectos sócio-economicos.** (Agriculture and animal husbandry in Macau: socio-economic aspects.)
Carlos Daniel de C. Batalha. Macau: Serviços Florestais e Agrícolas, [1984]. 76p. bibliog.

A discussion of changes in agriculture and animal husbandry since the 1950s is followed by an analysis of agricultural zones. Farming techniques, crops cultivated, animals reared, marketing procedures, and the local agricultural association are all discussed in detail. Although the book is essentially descriptive, there is some analysis of the flow of foreign agricultural goods into Macau and of agricultural intensity (through the use of a crop intensity index). Batalha documents the growing rôle of imported foods, the rapid decline of production, especially on the Macau peninsula, and the specialization of agriculture in high value fresh vegetable crops for the local market.

Transport

241 **Macau: relatório da Direcção dos Serviços das Obras Públicas 1932.**
(Macau: a report of the Directorate of the Public Works Department 1932.)
Artur Schiappa M. de Carvalho. Lisbon: Agência Geral das Colónias, 1935. 51p. map.

A report indicating construction undertaken by the Public Works Department from the late 1920s until 1932. Fifty-three photographs illustrate projects and buildings and the dredging of the ports is also discussed.

242 **Macau e o seu porto.** (Macau and its port.)
Eugénio Sanches da Gama. Lisbon: Agência Geral das Colónias, 1946. 30p.

First published in the *Boletim Geral das Colónias*, no. 253, much of this paper consists of an historical review of Macau given as a lecture at the Sociedade de Geografia de Lisboa in June 1946. Sanches da Gama emphasizes that Macau was not such a bad choice for a port for the 16th-century Portuguese as it now appears. Not only were the ships of that time smaller and the harbour calmer, but also the water depth was probably greater than in the 20th century. He gives a date of 1533 for the first anchoring of the Portuguese at Macau, but no source. Towards the end of his paper, he advocates the construction of a new port on Coloane.

243 **Obras do porto de Macau.** (Projects for the port of Macau.)
Antonio Pinto de Miranda Guedes. Macau: Imprensa Nacional, 1911. 58p.

Consists of revised notes of a lecture given at the Macau Military Club (Gremio Militar de Macau) on 25 July 1910. The author argues for the implementation of a definitive project to improve the Porto Interior. He compares a plan drawn up in 1908 with a similar project proposed in 1884. Harbour and shipping statistics for 1908 are included.

244   **O problema comercial e político de Portugal no Oriente.** (The
commercial and political problem of Portugal in the Orient.)
Tomé Pires (*pseud.*), Luís Nolasco.   Lisbon: Imprensa Nacional, 1925.
52p. 7 maps.

This set of four propaganda articles originally appeared in the Macau journal, *A Pátria*. The three initial articles urge the Portuguese to consider Asia, as well as Africa and Brazil, as a focus for colonial activities. Of most interest is the fourth article which traces the history of Macau and includes maps showing post-1926 plans for land reclamation and a railway from Macau to Guangzhou, which has not yet been built.

245   **Projecto das obras a executar no pôrto de Macau.** (Works project to be
implemented on the port of Macau.)
Portugal, Ministério das Colónias.   Lisbon: Imprensa Nacional, 1913.
272p. 2 maps.

A study for improving the port of Macau undertaken in response to increasing pressure for new port works after the 1883 Loureiro report. Includes much data about the condition of the port in 1910. Many recommendations, some of which were carried out, are mentioned, including land reclamation to the north and south of Ilha Verde, along the Porto Interior and the Praia Grande.

Statistics

246 **Síntese da evolução de alguns indicadores sócio-económicos 1981-1985.**
(A synthesis of the evolution of several socio-economic indicators 1981-1985).
Compiled by Gabinete do Secretário-Adjunto para a Coordenação
Económica. Macau: Governo de Macau, [1986]. 8p.
A brief summary of socio-economic trends in the territory accompanied by an
appendix of twenty-six tables. The text notes the strength of export-oriented light
industry and tourism in recent years. One section details the expansion of
communications, energy, transportation, and social welfare in the territory.

247 **Exportação especial por países: Special export by countries.**
J. Noronha. Macau: Serviços de Estatistica, 1976. 50p.
A bilingual table of statistics for exports to all countries from Macau. The table, which
is in patacas, covers the years 1966 to 1975 with thirty-eight colour bar graphs for
major trading partners. A turning away from trade with Portugese overseas territories
is apparent after 1970.

248 **Inquérito industrial 1980.** (Industrial inquiry 1980.)
Compiled by Repartição dos Serviços de Estatistica. Macau: Governo
de Macau, 1983. 185p.
Presents statistics for the 1,131 officially registered industries in Macau in 1980. The
text is in Portuguese and Chinese.

249 **Anuário estatístico: Yearbook of statistics.**
Compiled by Serviços de Estatística e Censos. Macau: Governo de
Macau. annual.
The best general source for statistics on Macau. Recent volumes include chapters on
geography and climate, demography, social security and welfare, education and

recreation, law and criminality, tourism, industry, energy, construction, foreign trade, consumer prices, money and finance, public finance, gross domestic product, and transport and communications. Comparisons for recent years are made in tabular form. Most of the recent tables are listed in Portuguese, English, and Chinese.

Macau: imagens e números. (Macau: images and numbers.)
See item no. 21.

Notas científicas. (Scientific notes.)
See item no. 23.

Resultados dos observações meterológicas de Macau. (Results of meterological observations of Macau.)
See item no. 24.

Saúde 85: Health '85.
See item no. 202.

Education

General

250 **A educação em Macau.** (Education in Macau.)
Manuel Teixeira. Macau: Direcção dos Serviços de Educação e
Cultura, 1982. 422p.
Presents a history of schools in Macau up to 1981, covering all education from primary
to tertiary level. Civic and religious schools are discussed separately and details are
provided on famous educators such as Graciete Agostinho Nogueira Batalha and Ana
Maria de Sousa Marques da Silva Amaro, A. M.

251 **Schooling in East Asia: forces of change; formal and nonformal
education in Japan, the Republic of China, the People's Republic of
China, South Korea, North Korea, Hong Kong, and Macau.**
Edited by R. Murray Thomas, T. Neville Postlethwaite. Oxford:
Pergamon, 1983. 350p. 5 maps. bibliog.
This book consists of chapters on the education system in the different territories of
East Asia. In the Macau chapter (p. 298-307), Thomas presents a general picture of
Macau's education system in the early 1980s. He notes the important rôle private
institutions play in Macau's education and the problems of competition between
Portuguese and English as a second language for Macau's Chinese population.

Primary and secondary systems

252 **Elementos de história de Macau.** (Elements of the history of Macau.)
Beatriz Basto da Silva. Macau: Direcção dos Serviços de Educação,
1986, vol. 1. 227p.
Presents basic materials and methods for teaching the history of Macau in Macau's
Portuguese language schools. The other three volumes in this series have yet to be
published, but will cover elementary Luso-Chinese teaching, a general secondary
course and a scholastic course.

253 **Esino em Macau; uma abordagem sistémica da realidade educativa.**
(Teaching in Macau; a systemic approach to an educational reality.)
M. Conceição Avles Pinto. Macau: Gabinete do Secretário-Adjunto
para a Educação e Cultura, 1987. 73p. bibliog.
For this study of primary and secondary students and teachers, the author draws on
data collected during 1984 and 1985. Teaching in the languages of Macau: Cantonese,
Portuguese, Luso-Chinese, English, and Anglo-Chinese leads to the creation of
separate educational systems with little intercommunication. On the Chinese side, the
author sees a need for better training of teachers, while the Portuguese teachers should
aim for greater cultural understanding of their Chinese students.

254 **Liceu de Macau.**
Manuel Teixeira. Macau: Dírecção dos Serviços de Educacão, 577p.
rev. ed. 1986.
First published in 1944 and corrected and augmented in 1969 and 1986, the book
outlines the origins of public instruction in Macau from the founding of the Colégio da
Madre de Deus in the 18th century. Teixeira discusses the founding of the Liceu, its
first teachers, problems faced by the school in its early years, organizations related to
the Liceu and the status of the Liceu within the Portuguese educational system. The
book concludes with short biographical sketches of some of its more famous teachers
including Camilo de Almeida Pessanha, Venceslau deMorais and Manuel de Silva
Mendes.

Pedro Nolasco da Silva. (Pedro Nolasco da Silva.)
See item no. 146.

Higher education

255 **University of Macau: Universidade de Macau.**
[Macau]: [n.p.], [1980]. 20p. 3 maps.
Describes the origins of the University of Macau which was soon renamed the
University of East Asia. This pamphlet includes sections on regional needs for higher
education, the proposed University estate, student hostels, the University's constitu-
tion, academic programmes, staff, admission, the rector and the planning board for
September 1980. This pamphlet has just been superseded by Bernard Mellor's *The
University of East Asia: origin and outlook* (Hong Kong: UEA Press, 1989) which is
the first official history of the University.

Literature

Literary history and criticism

256 **Poesia tradicional de Macau.** (Traditional poetry of Macau.)
Graciete Agostinho Nogueira Batalha.   Macau: Tipografia Marsul,
1988. 8p.
This is a corrected version of the text previously published in the journal *Macau* (q.v.),
no. 4 (August 1987), p.40–43. Batalha considers the style of the Portuguese language
poets of Macau and asserts that Maquista poetry has always been basically Portuguese
despite the modifications in dialect.

257 **Was Camoens ever in Macau?**
Charles Ralph Boxer.   *T'ien Hsia Monthly*, vol. 10, no. 4 (April 1940),
p. 324-33.
Contributes to the continuing debate on whether the famous poet, Luís Vaz de
Camões, ever visited Macau. Boxer is of the opinion that there is no conclusive
evidence either way but that it is highly unlikely that Camões ever wrote parts of his
epic poem, *Os Lusíadas* in the Camões Grotto at Macau.

258 **The Lusiads.**
Luís Vaz de Camões, translated and introduced by William C.
Atkinson.   Harmondsworth, England; Baltimore, Maryland: Penguin,
1952. 249p.
In his introduction to this translation of Portugal's epic poem, *Os Lusíadas*, the
translator states that Camões came to Macau in 1557 after being appointed to the post
of Trustee for the Dead and Absent in Macau. He does not mention that Camões'
presence in Macau has been the subject of much debate. The poem itself describes
Vasco da Gama's voyage to India but does not include any reference to Macau. In
Canto Ten (p. 218-49) a sea-goddess takes da Gama to the top of a high mountain and
tells him of the places in East Asia which the Portuguese will 'discover'. Macau is not
mentioned, perhaps because Camões considered it part of China.

259   **China (estudos e tradições).** (China: studies and traditions.)
Camilo de Almeida Pessanha.   Lisbon: Agência Geral das Colónias,
1944. 131p.
Although most of this book is concerned with Chinese literature and aesthetics,
Pessanha devotes one chapter to the significance of the Camões Grotto for the people
of Macau and the Portuguese nation. However, he believes that Camões probably
never visited Macau.

260   **Camões em Macau: contribuições para o estudo do problema.** (Camões
in Macau: contributions to the study of the problem.)
Manuel Teixeira.   Macau: Imprensa Nacional, 1940. 68p.
Refutes the theories of Gonçalo da Gama and Charles Ralph Boxer that the famous
Portuguese poet, Luís Vaz de Camões, probably never came to Macau. There is a final
note about the Camões Grotto in Macau. The information found in this book overlaps
with that found in Teixeira's later work, *Camões esteve em Macau* (q.v.).

261   **Camões esteve em Macau.** (Camões was in Macau.)
Manuel Teixera.   Macau: Direcção dos Serviços de Educação e
Cultura, 1981. 47p.
Supports the view that Luís Vaz de Camões visited Macau, although Teixeira is
convinced that the poet was not Trustee for the Dead and Absent as is often claimed,
since there is no documentary record of such a post in Macau until 1582.

20th-century trends and writers

262   **Chü Kóng.** (The Zhu Jiang or Pearl River.)
Maria do Rosário Almeida, preface by Túlio Tomás, introduced by
José dos Santos Ferreira.   Macau: Instituto Cultural, 1987. 81p.
Includes thirty poems about Macau and things Cantonese.

263   **Por caminhos solitários.** (By secluded pathways.)
Leonel Alves.   Macau: [n.p.], [1983]. 113p.
Comprises sixty-nine poems intimately connected with Macau.

264   **Cheong-sam (a cabaia).** (Cheong-sam: Chinese blouse.)
Deolinda do Carmo Salvado da Conceição.   Macau: Instituto Cultural,
1987. 3rd ed. 280p.
Presents a series of short stories about Chinese people and the struggle which they
have experienced.

265   **Amor e dedinhos de pé: romance de Macau.** (Love and dedinhos de pé:
a Macau novel.)
Henrique de Senna Fernandes.   Macau: Instituto Cultural, 1986, 383p.
This romantic novel draws on the people and customs of Macau for its setting.

266   **Nam Van contos de Macau.** (Nam Van: stories of Macau.)
      Henrique de Senna Fernandes.   Macau: Henrique de Senna
      Fernandes, [1978]. 158p.
Six short stories which take place in Macau or deal with themes related to Macau.

267   **História de Maria e Alferes João.** (The story of Maria and Alféris
      Juám.)
      José dos Santos Ferreira.   Macau: Instituto Cultural, 1987. 63p.
Presents a standard Portuguese edition of the romance entitled, in Maquista, *Estória di
Maria co Alféris Juám*, translated by the author.

268   **Macau di tempo antigo.** (The Macau of times past.)
      José dos Santos Ferreira, preface by Verónica Garizo.   Macau: The
      Author, 1985. 181p.
This selection of poems and a short novel in the Maquista dialect includes an extensive
Maquista/Standard Portuguese glossary.

269   **Macau sã assi.** (Macau is like this.)
      José dos Santos Ferreira.   Macau: Tipografia da Missão do Padroado,
      1967. 138p.
A collection of plays and poems, mostly written between 1953 and 1967, in the
Maquista dialect of Portuguese. A vocabulary list of Maquista words translated into
Standard Portuguese is included (p. 101-38).

270   **Poéma di Macau (poesia e prosa) – dialecto macaense.** (Poéma di Macau
      (poetry and prose) – in the Maquista dialect.)
      José dos Santos Ferreira, preface by Túlio Lopes Tomás.   Macau: Leal
      Senado, 1983. 277p.
A selection of literary pieces, largely poems, in the Maquista dialect with an
introduction by Santos Ferreira about the state of the dialect and his reason for
compiling Maquista poetry. Included are Christmas carols in Maquista.

271   **Qui-nova Chencho.** (What's new Chencho.)
      José dos Santos Ferreira, preface by José Silveira Machado.   Macau:
      Tipografia da Missão do Padroado, 1973. 208p.
A collection of poems and plays in the Maquista dialect. 'Qui-nova Chencho' is the
name of a play included in this volume which was first performed in Macau in 1969.

272   **Macau factos e lendas – páginas escolhida.** (Macau: facts and legends –
      selected pages.)
      Luís Gonzaga Gomes, preface by Graciete Agostinho Noguiera
      Batalha.   Lisbon: Quinzena de Macau, 1979. 149p. bibliog.
Presents a collection of writings by the Macaense author, Luís Gonzaga Gomes (1907-
76) who wrote about such diverse topics as history, politics, sports, music, and Macau.
This volume contains nineteen anecdotal works about places and customs in Macau.

273   **Novos territórios.** (New territories.)
       Jorge Listopad.   Macau: Instituto Cultural, 1986. 18p.
Offers impressions of Macau, China, Hong Kong and related topics in the form of
several short sketches.

274   **Colectânea de artigos de Manuel da Silva Mendes.** (A collection of
       articles by Manuel da Silva Mendes.)
       Manuel da Silva Mendes, compiled by Luís Gonzaga Gomes.   Macau:
       Notícias de Macau, 1963-64. 4 vols. (Colecção *Notícias de Macau*, nos.
       XVIII, XIX, XX, XXI).
These articles were collected largely from Macau newspapers. Dr. Manuel da Silva
Mendes (1876-1931) resided in Macau, except for visits to Portugal, from 1901 until his
death. In addition to his work as a teacher of Portuguese and Latin at the Liceu
Nacional de Macau, he was also a lawyer and a collector of Chinese art. Volume one,
Arte, contains articles concerned with architecture and painting in Macau and China as
well as aspects of Daoist (Taoist) philosophy. Volume two, *Problemas citadinos*, is a
collection of a wide range of articles covering social issues such as water supply, low-
cost housing, and education. Articles on aspects of Chinese life, including observations
on Chinese philosophy and notes on famous Portuguese individuals and events in East
Asia make up volume three, *Assuntos sínicos e crónicas*. The last volume, *Diversos*,
includes a long text on Macau published posthumously as well as an article describing
Mendes' funeral.

275   **Macau impressões e recordações.** (Macau: impressions and
       recollections.)
       Manuel da Silva Mendes, preface by Graciete Agostinho Noguiera
       Batalha.   Lisbon: Quinzena de Macau. 1979. 131p.
This collection of seventeen articles on Macau and Chinese culture in the territory,
provides a smaller selection than that found in *Colectânea de artigos de Manuel da Silva
Mendes*. (A collection of articles by Manuel da Silva Mendes.) (q.v.). However, these
seventeen articles are perhaps most representative of the Macau that Mendes knew.

276   **Sobre filosofia.** (On philosophy.)
       Manuel da Silva Mendes.   Macau: Leal Senado, 1983. 169p.
Twenty-five short essays and poems explore the subjects of temples in Macau and
Daoist (Taoist) philosophy. This collection was compiled from a range of sources
including public lectures and Macau journals.

277   **História dum soldado.** (The story of a soldier.)
       José Joaquim Monteiro.   Macau: Direcção dos Serviços de Turismo,
       1983. 4th ed. 39p.
Presents poems written in 1940 by a long-term Portuguese resident of Macau.
Monteiro was a soldier in Macau from 1937 to 1946 and has worked in the education
department of the Macau government since 1951.

278 **Macau vista por dentro.** (Macau seen from the inside.)
    José Joaquim Monteiro.   Macau: Direcção dos Serviços de Turismo,
    1983. 385p. map.
A book of poetry, twenty-four years in the making, which focuses on the history,
landscape, monuments, legends, costumes, holidays, foods and other activities of
Macau.

279 **De volta a Macau.** (Back to Macau.)
    José Joaquim Monteiro.   Macau: Direcção dos Serviços de Turismo,
    1983. 2nd ed. 126p.
A collection of poems first published in 1952 after Monteiro returned to Macau from
Portugal. The poems trace the poet's voyage from Portugal to Macau via many points
in the former Portuguese empire. The style is melancholy and displays the poet's
passion for East Asia.

280 **Infraestructuras.** (Infrastructures.)
    Alberto Estima de Oliveira, introduced by Maria Alexandre.   Macau:
    Instituto Cultural, 1987. 67p.
A collection of twenty-six poems exploring the nature of symbolism.

281 **Inspirações.** (Inspirations.)
    Henrique Manuel Vizeu Pinheiro.   Macau: Imprensa Nacional. 1950.
    83p.
A collection of very brief essays written between 1923 and 1950, mostly during the time
that the author was in Macau. Many are sentimental and patriotic, but some describe
incidents which occurred in Macau.

282 **Espelho do mar.** (A mirror of the sea.)
    Benjamim Antonio Videira Pires.   Macau: Instituto Cultural, 1986.
    57p.
Presents a collection of twenty-six poems by a long-term resident and historian.

283 **Luís Gonzaga Gomes uma vida.** (Luís Gonzaga Gomes: a life.)
    Manuel Teixeira.   Macau: Instituto Cultural, 1986. [16p.].
Comments on the work of Luís Gonzaga Gomes and provides a list of Gomes' books
and articles. There is also an appended list of titles for a phot-exhibition for which this
pamphlet was issued.

284 **Histórias de Macau.** (Stories of Macau.)
    Antino do Tojal.   Lisbon: Edições Rolim. 1987. 395p.
This collection of thirty-seven short stories has Macau as its backdrop. Much of the
detail owes more to the author's imagination than to the reality of life in the territory.

285 **Macau jardim abençoado.** (Macau a blessed garden.)
José dos Santos Ferriera. Macau: Instituto Cultural, 1988. 181p.
Offers poetry and prose in the Maquista dialect with a standard Portuguese translation
for most of the poems.

286 **Fotobiografia de Deolinda Salvado da Conceição.** (A photobiography of
Delinda do Carmo Salvado da Conceição.)
Introduced by António Conceição Júnior, José dos Santos Ferriera.
Macau: Instituto Cultural, 1987. [37p.]
Notes about the author and journalist are followed by thirty-two black-and-white
photos depicting her life.

Historical and popular novels

287 **City of broken promises.**
Austin Coates. Hong Kong, Singapore, Kuala Lumpur: Heinemann
Asia, 1977. 313p. (Reprinted Hong Kong: Oxford University Press,
1988, 320p.)
A novel set in Macau from 1780 to 1798 and based on the life of Martha Merop (1766-
1828), the property of Thomas Kuyck van Merop, an Englishman of Anglo-Dutch
parentage. When Thomas arrived in Macau, Martha came with his house. After having
been sold into prostitution at thirteen she went on to become a trader in her own right
and one of the richest women on the China coast.

288 **Macau.**
Daniel Carney. London: Corgi, 1986. 432p.
A popular novel of fantasy and adventure which uses Macau as a 'city of sin' for its
background.

289 **Rendez-vous à Macao.** (A rendez-vous at Macau.)
Jean Graton. Brussells: Graton éditeur, 1983. 48p.
A comic-book adventure, including crashes during the Macau Grand Prix and *gōngfū*
(kungfu) fighting. The drawings of Macau are remarkably authentic for literature of
this kind.

The Arts

Architecture

290 Old Macau.
Tom Briggs, Colin Crisswell.   Hong Kong: South China Morning Post,
1984. 96p. map.
Presents a collection of sketches, many of them in water colour, of thirty-three of
Macau's most famous landmarks with accompanying brief descriptions.

291 Chronicles in stone.
Shann Davies.   Macau: Department of Tourism, 1985. 132p.
Considers twenty historical buildings and monuments and the part that they played in
the life of Macau. Each of these well-illustrated essays originally appeared in various
issues of *Macau Travel Talk* (q.v.)

292 Macau cultural heritage: Património arquitectónico Macau.
Francisco Figueira, Carlos Marreiros.   Macau: Instituto Cultural,
1988. 283p. 3 maps.
A collection of 455 photographs which shows the architecture of Macau as a mixture of
Chinese, Portuguese and foreign elements. These photographs were part of an
exhibition held in Lisbon, Paris and Macau. The photographs are grouped under the
following topics: the city, Chinese architecture, the Praia Grande, the São Lázaro
district, Avenida Almeida Ribeiro, churches, stately homes, art deco heritage,
gardens, lost heritage and preserved heritage. Another book compiled by Francisco
Figueira and Adalberto Tenreiro, *Os últimos dez anos, arquitectos em Macau* (The last
ten years, architects in Macau) (Macau: Instituto Cultural, 1986. 111p.) covers
architectural work from 1976 to 1986. Colour photographs show the architects and
their designs and some technical data on the buildings is provided.

293 **Fortifications of Macau, their design and history.**
Jorge Graça. Macau: Direcção dos Serviços de Turismo, 1984. 2nd
ed. 132p. 29 maps. bibliog.
Traces the historical and geographical development of Macau's fortresses in three
periods: 1557-1622, 1622-38 and 1849-84. Graça discusses the objective of each fort as
well as the design and materials used for construction. A Portuguese translation of this
text with many colour plates was published by the Instituto Cultural de Macau in 1987
under the title, *Fortificações de Macau: concepção e história.*

294 **An architectural survey of the Jesuit seminary church of St. Paul's,**
Macao.
Michael Hugo-Brunt. *Journal of Oriental Studies*, vol. 1, no. 2 (July
1954), p. 327-44.
A short history of the mission movement in Macau is followed by a detailed history
and an architectural survey of the São Paulo church. The text is accompanied by
sixteen plates including excellent drawings of the façade by architectural students at the
University of Hong Kong, undertaken in 1952. This article was reissued by Hong Kong
University Press (1955).

295 **The convent and church of St. Dominic at Macao.**
Michael Hugo-Brunt, José Maria Braga. *Journal of Oriental Studies*,
vol. 4, nos. 1-2 (1957-58), p. 66-78. 2 maps.
This article, which was reissued by Hong Kong University Press (1961), discusses the
early history of the convent and church of São Domingos. The plan of the church, its
façade, sides and interior, as well as its site, are all described. The article is illustrated
by a series of twelve black-and-white plates, including photographs, a map and six
sketches of the church from various angles.

296 **The parish church of St. Lawrence at Macao.**
Michael Hugo-Brunt. *Journal of Oriental Studies*, vol. 6,
nos. 1-2 (1961-64), p. 109-14. map.
A brief history of the site and buildings of the São Lourenço church is followed by an
architectural description and twelve black-and-white plates. The plates include
photographs, plans, and sketches. This article was reissued by Hong Kong University
Press (1967).

297 **Traces of Chinese and Portuguese architecture.**
Carlos Marreiros. In: *Macau: city of commerce and culture.* Edited by
Rolf Dieter Cremer. Hong Kong: UEA Press, 1987, p. 87-102. bibliog.
Relates the development of Chinese and Portuguese architectural styles in Macau,
considers their mingling to create some unique buildings, and notes recent efforts to
preserve Macau's architectural heritage.

298 **Bela Vista Hotel.**
Manuel Teixeira. Macau: Centro de Informação e Turismo, 1978.
28p.

A bilingual pamphlet in English and Portuguese which describes the changes in ownership and use of this charming building during its 100 years' existence. Included are eight black-and-white photographs of the hotel.

299 **The church of St. Paul in Macau.**
Manuel Teixeira. Lisbon: Centro de Estudos Históricos Ultramarinos da Junta de Investigações do Ultramar, 1979. [60p.]

First published in *Studia*, nos. 41-42 (Jan./Dec. 1979), this text provides a detailed history and architectural description of the most famous landmark of Macau. Schools and hospitals associated with São Paulo's as well as benefactors are also mentioned. Further information can be found in *A fachada de S. Paulo*, (The façade of São Paulo church) also by Manuel Teixeira (Macau: Imprensa Nacional, 1941. 57p.), which concludes with a comparison to several churches in Lisbon.

300 **Residência dos governadores de Macau.** (The residence of the governors of Macau.)
Manuel Teixeira. Macau: Direcção dos Serviços de Turismo e Communicação Social, [1980]. 51p.

Discusses the movements of the Governor's residence and the seat of government throughout the years. The current seat of government on the Praia Grande (Palácio da Praia Grande) only dates from 1884. Before this date, Governors lived in palaces along the Praia Grande and in various residences given them by the Leal Senado. Included are colour photographs of the Palácio da Praia Grande, the Governor's residence first used for this purpose in 1926, Santa Sancha, and the fort of São Paulo.

301 **The story of Ma-kok-miu.**
Manuel Teixeira. Macau: Centro de Informação e Turismo, 1979.
77p.

The title on the outer cover of this book is *The Chinese Temple of Barra*. Teixeira gives various interpretations of the founding of the Má Kók Temple and describes it in detail. The texts of some Chinese essays found carved on the rocks are appended and translated into English by Dr. Paul Clasper and Dominic Yip.

302 **Macao ou jouer la différence.** (Macau: building the difference.)
Edited by Anne de la Vasselais, Madeleine Villalta. Paris: Centre Georges Pompidou, Centre de Création Industrielle, 1983. 96p. 4 maps.

A well-illustrated book presenting Macau's archictectural heritage as a mixture of Portuguese and Chinese cultures with a distinct emphasis on the Portuguese aspects. Macau's geographical and historical development is also summarized and the territory is contrasted with Hong Kong in a collection of brief essays.

Leal Senado. (The Loyal Senate.)
See item no. 137.

Visual Arts

303 **Alguns aspectos de artesanato em Macau.** (Several aspects of industrial arts in Macau.)
Ana Maria de Sousa Marques da Silva Amaro.   Macau: Centro do Informação e Turismo, 1967. 47p.

Presents an illustrated discussion of the Chinese-style artisans of Macau and their work. Discussed in order of importance are bamboo objects, firecrackers, paper crafts, joss sticks, candles for worship, woodwork, cloth decorations, lamps, feather dusters, rope, fishing implements, rattan and plastic furniture, metal plated objects, bronze pieces, match boxes, glass and mirror paintings, figures made from baked flour, coconut shell spoons, items made from plastic ribbon, wooden clogs, bonsai plants, children's clothes, mahjong pieces, and weaving.

304 **O jardim de Lou Lim Ieóc.** (The Lou Lim Ieóc garden.)
Ana Maria de Sousa Marques da Silva Amaro.   Macau: Imprensa Nacional, 1967. 44p. 8 maps.

An introduction to Chinese gardens is followed by a detailed account of the history and layout of this most famous of Macau's gardens. The pamphlet is well illustrated with photographs of the garden in the past and in 1967, with maps showing the modifications made in the garden's layout between 1920 and 1963, and with drawings of fresco motifs.

305 **George Chinnery 1774-1852: artist of the China coast.**
Henry Berry-Hill, Sidney Berry-Hill, forward by Alice Winchester.
Leigh-on-Sea, England: F. Lewis, 1963. 63p. bibliog.

One of the earliest full-length books on Chinnery, it covers his life in Macau in Chapters V-IX (p. 37-61). Plates 30-75 include many scenes of Macau and portraits painted in Macau.

306 **Pintura de Anabela Canas e Lei Chan Fu.** (The painting of Anabela Canas and Lei Chan Fu.)   Macau: Instituto Cultural, 1988. [12p.].

This catalogue of paintings by two Macau artists was published to accompany an exhibition held at the Livraria Portuguesa in Macau during March 1988.

307 **A catalogue of Chinese paintings in the Luis de Camoes Museum Macau.**
Compiled by Helen Ho Chan.   Macau: Imprensa Nacional, 1977. 67p. bibliog. (Centre of Asian Studies Bibliographies and Research Guides, no. 11).

Comprises a catalogue of 216 paintings by forty-three Guangdong artists. The collection started with the acquisition of the Chinese art collection of Dr. Manuel da Silva Mendes (1876-1931) in 1931. Fifty-four black-and-white plates are included in the catalogue.

308 **Macau as viewed by some of its artists: Macau vista por alguns dos seus artistas.**
Edited by Direcção dos Serviços de Turismo. Macau: The Author, [1987]. 2nd ed. 96p.

A collection of colour photographs and paintings showing many aspects of Macau. All the illustrations have titles in Portuguese, Chinese and English.

309 **'China trade' paintings: Pinturas da 'China trade'.**
Introduced by Cesar Guillen-Nuñez. Macau: Instituto Cultural, [1986]. [56p.]

An introduction to the Western-style China trade paintings of the mid-19th century, presented in Portuguese, Chinese and English and accompanied by over fifty colour illustrations.

310 **Macau through the eyes of nineteenth century painters.**
Cesar Guillen-Nuñez. In: *Macau: city of commerce and culture*. Edited by Rolf Dieter Cremer. Hong Kong: UEA Press, 1987, p. 53-69. bibliog.

This article concentrates on representations of Macau's landscape with particular emphasis on George Chinnery (1774-1852) and Auguste Borget (1808-1877).

311 **Souvenirs of Auguste Borget.**
Robin G. Hutcheon. Hong Kong: South China Morning Post, 1979. 123p. bibliog.

Borget's six month stay in Macau is covered in a chapter entitled 'Macau, Manila, India' (p.93-99). At the end of the book are plates of Borget's original paintings with copies by Thomas Allom.

312 **Chinnery: the man and the legend.**
Robin G. Hutcheon, Geoffrey W. Bonsall. Hong Kong: South China Morning Post, 1975. 158p. 2 maps. bibliog.

The story of Chinnery and his links with Macau where he spent most of his time from 1825 to his death in 1852. The Macau years are covered in chapters seven to thirteen (p. 53-131). Colour plates include many scenes of Macau.

313 **Painters of Macau: Pintores de Macau.**
Edited by Instituto Cultural de Macau. Macau: The Author, 1987.

Comprises two folders of postcards issued to introduce the painters of Macau to the outside world. The folders contain a brief explanation of the purpose of the collections and the names of the artists and their works in Portuguese, Chinese, and English. One folder of 'Oriental Paintings' contains twelve paintings and four examples of Chinese caligraphy by eight artists while the other folder of 'Western Painting' includes twenty-four works by twelve painters.

314   **Macau by Jane O'neill.**
      Jane O'neill.   Hong Kong: Macau Mokes, 1987. 6 plates.
Jane O'neill is a British artist who made pen-and-ink drawings of Macau in 1985. This is a limited edition set of six drawings including studies of the façade of São Paulo church, the Macau Military Club and the memorial home of Dr. Sun Yat-sen. Two drawings of buildings on the Avenida do Conselheiro Ferreira de Almeida and a street scene from Coloane village are also included in the collection.

315   **The Chater Collection: pictures relating to China, Hong Kong and Macao, 1665-1860; with historical and descriptive letterpress.**
      James Orange.   London: Thornton Butterworth, 1924. 528p. bibliog.
The section on Macau (p. 275-319) presents anecdotes about the territory and prints of forty-three Western China trade paintings dating from 1655 to 1850 with accompanying catalogue notes. Included are works by George Chinnery, Auguste Borget, Thomas Allom and Marciano Baptista.

316   **Macao.**
      Bernard C Schoenfeld, Stanley Rubin.   New York: Frederick Ungar, 1980. 81p.
The screenplay for the 1952 film 'Macao', directed by Josef von Sternberg, is accompanied by pictures of Robert Mitchum, Jane Russell and other stars in scenes from the movie. This film exemplifies the popular image of Macau in the English-speaking world as a 'sin city'.

317   **George Chinnery no bicentenário do seu nascimento 1774-1974.** (George Chinnery on the bicentenary of his birth 1774-1974.)
      Manuel Teixeira.   Macau: Imprensa Nacional, 1974. 122p. bibliog.
In this life story of George Chinnery, Teixeira offers some corrections to the Berry-Hills' biography (q.v.), for instance, the fact that the artist never visited Sri Lanka (then Ceylon) or Shanghai. Illustrations of some famous paintings are appended with comments on Chinnery's students, Lam Kua and Marciano Baptista.

Macau.
See item no. 8.

Performing arts

318   **O brinco do leão.** (The game of the lion.)
      Ana Maria de Sousa Marques da Silva Amaro.   Macau: Direcçao dos Serviços de Turismo, 1984. 204p. bibliog.
An historical analysis and description of the processions, masks, and movements of traditional Chinese martial arts as practised in Macau. Considerable emphasis is given to the lion dance and resumés in English, French, German and Chinese are provided.

319   **De Alcafache a Macau.** (From Alcafache to Macau.)
      Abel Moura.   Macau: Instituto Cultural, 1987. 70p.
This book of Portuguese popular music contains lyrics and scores. Macau is the place
of origin of the last three songs in the book (p. 56-63).

Customs, costume and cuisine

320   **A cozinha macaense.** (A Macaense cuisine.)
      Maria Margarida Gomes.   Macau: Imprensa Nacional, 1984. 24p.
A brief account of the origins of Macaense cuisine followed by descriptions of thirty-
three Macaense dishes. Included are comments on eating customs for these dishes, but,
unfortunately, no recipes are provided.

321   **Bons petiscos.** (Good delacacies.)
      Maria Celestina de Mello e Senna.   Macau: Direcção dos Serviços de
      Turismo, 1983, 3rd ed. 127p.
This book of Macaense recipes includes dishes which were created over a century ago.
The entries are divided into sweets, salty dishes, and Macaense entrées (cozinhados de
Macau).

322   **A fénix e o dragão realidade e mito do casamento chinês.** (The phoenix
      and the dragon: reality and myth in Chinese marriages.)
      Cecilia Jorge, Beltrão Coelho.   Macau: Instituto Cultural, 1988. 157p.
      bibliog.
Although this book discusses Chinese wedding customs in general, there is a distinct
emphasis on Chinese-style weddings in Macau. The photographs are of Macau
weddings and one section is devoted specifically to the legal aspects of marriage in
Macau.

Os Chins de Macau. (The Chinese of Macau.)
See item no. 164.

Macau e os seus habitantes: relações com Timor. (Macau and its residents:
relations with Timor.)
See item no. 161.

Sports and Recreation

Gambling

323 **O jogo em Macau.** (Gambling in Macau.)
Governo de Macau.   Macau: Inspecção dos Contratos de Jogos, 1985.
310p.
This introduction to the history of gambling and casinos in Macau is followed by an explanation of the rules of the major games and a classification of the casinos. The social, economic, and political aspects of Macau's gambling industry are discussed in separate chapters. Approximately 200 pages are devoted to appendices which describe casinos in other countries, provide statistical analyses of winning probabilities, and list the laws relating to Macau's gambling concessions.

324 **Gamblers guide to Macao.**
B. Okuley, F. King-Poole.   Hong Kong: South China Morning Post,
1979. 104p.
In its day, this was a good guide to all forms of gambling in Macau. The book starts with a history of gambling in Macau and a profile of the men who created the industry. This introduction is followed by an explanation of some of the major gambling games found in Macau. Another chapter entitled 'What else in Macao' explains some of the tourist attractions found in the territory. There is an appendix on the Happy Valley race track in Hong Kong (p. 92-194).

325 **Roulette for the millions.**
Patrick O'Neal-Dunne.   London: Sidgwick & Jackson, 1971. 204p.
This chatty account relates the adventures of a roulette player and his beautiful secretary who, with five others, supposedly ran the longest roulette game ever in the Casino Lisboa in 1969. The roulette played in Macau is described in detail and some of the personal aspects of Macau's gambling industry in the late 1960s are revealed. The description of Macau is, however, very general.

326 **Gambling in Macau.**
António Duarte de Almeida Pinho. In: *Macau: city of commerce and culture.* Edited by Rolf Dieter Cremer. Hong Kong: UEA Press, 1987, p. 155-64. bibliog.
Provides a brief history of gambling, an assessment of its economic impact in Macau and an analysis of the types of gambling practised in the territory. Pinho notes the effect of Chinese customs on Macau's gambling industry.

Thrilling cities.
See item no. 79.

Other recreation

327 **Jogos, brinquedos e outras diversões populares de Macau.** (Games, toys and other popular diversions of Macau.)
Ana Maria de Sousa Marques da Silva Amaro. Macau: Imprensa Nacional, 1972. 510p. bibliog.
This detailed and well-illustrated account of children's diversions in Macau includes games, toys and songs. The traditions behind these diversions are traced to China, Europe (especially Portugal) India, Malacca and Timor.

328 **Três jogos populares de Macau: chonca, talu, bafá.** (Three popular games of Macau: chonca, talu and bafá.)
Ana Maria de Sousa Marques da Silva Amaro. Macau: Instituto Cultural, 1984. 107p. bibliog.
Amaro discusses three old Macaense games: chonca, which is African in origin; talu, which comes from Portugal; and bafá, a card game which originated in China. Resumés of the text are provided in Portuguese, French, English, German and Chinese.

329 **The maximaphily of Macao: A maximafilia de Macau: La maximaphilie de Macao.**
José António Duarte Martins. Macau: The Author, 1984. 205p.
A catalogue of postcards with stamps on the picture side. Martins provides dates for the first issue of the postcards and gives their value in French francs. The text is in Portuguese, Chinese, French and English.

330 **Macau postage stamps catalogue: Catálogo de selos de Macau.**
Edited by Kong Iat Cheong. Macau: Instituto Cultural, 1987. 117p.
A colour catalogue in English, Chinese and Portuguese which describes and evaluates stamps issued between 1884 and 1986.

O brinco do leão. (The game of the lion.)
See item no. 318.

O jardim de Lou Lim Ieóc. (The Lou Lim Ieoc garden.)
See item no. 304.

Libraries, Art Galleries, Museums and Archives

331 **Arquivos de Macau: Boletim do Arquivo Histórico de Macau.** (Macau Archives: Bulletin of the Historical Archives of Macau.)
Macau: Imprensa Nacional, Instituto Cultural, 1929- ; current series 1981- . bi-annual.
This bulletin provides an inventory of Macau's historical archives and some occasional articles.

332 **Documentos sobre a história da China.** (Documents on Chinese history.)
Macau: Instituto Cultural, Biblioteca Nacional, Biblioteca Sir Robert Ho Tung, 1987. 32p.
This bilingual Chinese and Portuguese bibliography contains fifty-five items on Chinese history from the Biblioteca Sir Robert Ho Tung in Macau.

333 **Maritime Museu of Macau: Museu Marítimo de Macau.**
Edited by Museu Marítimo de Macau. Macau: The Author, 1988. 31p.
Contains a brief introduction to the museum and colour illustrations of its displays. Captions are in English, Japanese, and Portuguese.

Exposição bibliográfica e documental.
See item no. 377.

De Portugal ao Extremo Oriente, exposição bibliográfica.
See item no. 379.

Book Production, Past and Present

334 **The beginnings of printing at Macau.**
José Maria Braga. *Studia*, no. 12 (July 1963), p. 29-137. bibliog.
Braga discusses the beginnings of printing in Macau in 1588 and the reintroduction of printing to the territory in 1815 by the British East India Company. Examples of early printing, such as the first newspaper, *A Abelha da China* (1823) and the *Gazeta de Macau* (1826), are also discussed. Appendices list books printed in Macau and Japan between 1588 and 1834. This is a substantially expanded and revised work based on Braga's earlier article: *O início da imprensa em Macau* (Macau: Escola Tipográfica do Orfanato, 1938. 26p.)

335 **Imprensa periódica portuguesa no Extremo Oriente.** (The Portuguese periodic press in East Asia.)
Manuel Teixeira. Macau: Notícias de Macau, 1965. 331p. (Colleccão *Notícias de Macau*, no XXII.)
This text is divided into two parts for 'Journalism in Macau' and 'Portuguese journalism in East Asia'. In part one, all newspapers and magazines published in Macau in Portuguese and English since the early 19th century are considered individually. Part two gives details relating to publications in Portuguese in Hong Kong, Guangzhou, Shanghai, Singapore, Malacca, Kôbe, Timor and Hawaii.

The relations between Portugal and Japan.
See item no. 101.

Periodicals and Mass Media

Newspapers

336 **Chêng Pou.** (Zhēng Bào.) (The Truth.)
Macau: Jornal Desportivo, 1978-. daily.
A four-page Chinese language paper.

337 **O Clarim.** (The Bugle.)
Macau: Semanário Católico, 1948-. weekly.
The contents of this Catholic newspaper focus on the rôle of the Church in the world and on religious cultural topics.

338 **O Comércio de Macau.** (The Macau Commerce Journal.)
Macau: Sociedade Editorial, 1987-. daily.
This Portuguese language daily, comprising approximately twenty-four pages, concentrates on commerce.

339 **Correio de Macau.** (The Macau Daily.)
Macau: 1982-. daily.
A Portuguese language paper.

340 **Expresso do Oriente.** (The Express of the Orient.)
Macau: Expresso Edições, 1989-. weekly.
This Portuguese language paper, of over twenty pages in length, has an emphasis on Macau's politics.

341 **Gazeta Macaense.** (The Macaense Gazette.)
Macau: 1963-. daily.
A Portuguese language paper.

342 **Jornal de Macau.** (The Journal of Macau.)
Macau, 1982-. daily.
A Portuguese evening paper of around twelve pages which includes television listings and sports coverage.

343 **Ou Mun Yât Pou.** (Aòmén Rìbào.) (Macau Daily News.)
Macau: 1958-. daily.
Macau's largest circulation Chinese paper, it has very clear connections with Beijing.

344 **Sân Hei.** (Chén Xǐ.) (Aurora.)
Macau: Secretaria do Diocesano de Coordenação, 1989-. [weekly].
A Catholic Chinese language newsletter.

345 **Sêng Pou.** (Xing Bào.) (Jornal 'Sing Pao'.) (The Star.)
Macau: 1963-. daily.
This Chinese language daily has a circulation of around 5,000.

346 **Si Mân Yât Pou.** (Shìmín Rìbào.) (Jornal do 'Cidadão'.) (The Citizen.)
Macau: Si Mân Pou Yip Kông Si, 1944-. daily.
A four-page Chinese language daily.

347 **Tái Chông Pou: Tai Chung Pou – Diário para Todos.** (Dàzhòng Bào.)
(Tai Chung Pou: the Daily for Everyone.)
Macau: Tái Chông Pou Yip Kông Si, 1933-. daily.
Macau's only newspaper in Chinese and Portuguese, it has a circulation of about 8,000 copies. A special edition is published for neighbouring Zhuhai. Specific topics are featured in special issues during the week.

348 **Today Macau: Yin Tói Ou Mun** (Xiàndài Aòmèn.)
Macau: [1987]-. weekly.
Macau's newest English and Chinese bilingual paper, it is about eight pages in length.

349 **Tribuna de Macau.** (The Macau Tribune.)
Macau: 1982-. weekly.
A quality journal which includes a magazine on the arts and a television magazine.

350 **Wá K'iu Pou.** (Húaqiáo Bào.) (Jornal 'Va Kio')
Macau: 1937-. daily.
Wá K'iu Pou began with strong connections to the Chinese Nationalist Party and was actually an offshoot of a paper by the same name in Hong Kong. With a circulation of about 35,000, it is the second most popular Chinese newspaper in Macau, after *Ou Mun Yât Pou* (q.v.).

General periodicals

351 **Macau.**
Macau: Gabinete de Communicação Social do Governo de Macau, 1987- . monthly.

This Portuguese language journal is the best source for up-to-date photographs of the territory. Its articles cover Macau, East Asia, and the Portuguese in Asia. *Macau* has a circulation of about 5,000 copies.

352 **Macau Image.**
Macau: Government of Macau, Directorate of Economic Services, 1985-. irregular.

A colour photo-magazine which promotes Macau's products. Included are the addresses of manufacturers.

353 **Nam Van.** (Nam Wan.)
Macau: Gabinete de Communicação Social do Governo de Macau, 1984-86. monthly.

Predecessor to the journal *Macau* (q.v.), the twenty-five issues of this journal have almost the same format and quality as the more recent magazine.

354 **Portuguese and Colonial Bulletin.**
London: K. Shingler, 1961-72. quarterly. irregular.

A leftist anti-Salazar pamphlet which included information about wars of independence in Portuguese Africa. There are a few notes referring to Macau during the anti-Portuguese demonstration of the Cultural Revolution era (1966-1976), mostly in the 1967 issues.

Imprensa periódica portuguesa no Extremo Oriente. (The Portuguese periodic press in East Asia.)
See item no. 335.

Macau Travel Talk.
See item no. 50

Professional, official and cultural periodicals

355 **Administração: Hâng Chêng.** (Xíng Zhèng.) (Administration.)
Macau: Serviço de Administração e Função Pública, 1988- . bi-annual.
This journal is devoted to the public administration of Macau. All articles appear in both Chinese and Portuguese.

356 **Boletim Bibliográfico de Macau.** (Bibliographical Bulletin of Macau.)
Macau: Instituto Cultural, Biblioteca Nacional, 1988-.
A series of bibliographical monographs which updates the *Bibliografia macaense* (q.v.). Entries are classified according to topics.

357 **Boletim do Instituto Luís Camões.** (Bulletin of the Luís Camões Institute.)
Macau: Instituto Luís de Camões, 1966-1980.
This journal, relating to cultural history, has an emphasis on Portuguese involvement in Macau.

358 **Bulletin of the Centre for Maritime Studies of Macau: Boletim do Centro de Estudos Marítimos de Macau.**
Macau: Centro de Estudos Marítimos, 1988-.
Naval topics form the main focus of this journal in Portuguese, Chinese and English.

359 **Journal of Macau Studies: Boletim de Estudos de Macau.**
Macau: Universidade da Ásia Oriental, 1988-.
Composed of articles, largely in Chinese, on various topics concerned with Macau, including economics and politics.

360 **Portuguese Studies Newsletter.**
Edited by Douglas L. Wheeler. Durham, New Hampshire: International Conference Group on Portugal, 1976-.
Although most of the information in the newsletter is about Portugal, new literature on Macau is mentioned in the book list section under 'Portuguese Asia'.

361 **Boletim Oficial.** (The Official Bulletin.)
Macau: Governo de Macau, 1838-. weekly.
The official bulletin of the Macau government which contains all the new laws and decrees from both Macau and Portugal which are relevant to the governing of the territory. The *Boletim Oficial* is received by all Macau government organizations and distributed to major libraries overseas.

Periodicals and Mass Media. Professional, official and cultural periodicals

362 **Review of Culture.**
Macau: Instituto Cultural, 1987-. quarterly.
Presents essays, poems and notes on various cultural topics. This journal is also available in Chinese and Portuguese editions.

363 **Religião e Pátria.** (Religion and Country.)
Macau, 1914-1968.
Contains contributions of an historical, religious and literary nature.

364 **Renascimento.** (Renascence.)
Macau, 1943-1945.
Contains contributions of an historical and literary nature.

Arquivos de Macau: Boletim do arquivo histórico de Macau. (Macau archives: Bulletin of the historical archives of Macau.)
See item no. 331.

Boletim Eclesial. (Ecclesiastical bulletin.)
See item no. 181.

Directories

365 **Anuário de Macau.** (Macau yearbook.)
Edited by Centro de Informação e Turismo. Macau: Imprensa
Nacional, [1949-1973]. annual.
Although it ceased publication in the early 1970s, this was the all-purpose reference
book for Macau during the 'provincial' post-World War II years. The yearbook
contains information on all aspects of government and provides lists of government
offices, education and health services, commercial, industrial, religious and charitable
institutions and their personnel.

366 **Ou Mun sâu ch'ák.** (Aùmén shǒucè.) (Macau handbook.)
Edited by Ou Mun Yât Pou (Aòmén Rìbao). Macau: The Author,
1983. 191p. map.
Issued by the Ou Mun Yât Pou (Macau Daily News) on its 25th anniversary, the
handbook opens with a general description of Macau and a display of colour
photographs of Zhuhai and Macau. After a section on the territory's laws, there follow
lists of inns, restaurants, construction firms, banking firms, jewellers, department
stores, tourist agencies, industries, doctors, social organizations, and schools. Bus
routes and meteorological phenomena are also described. The whole handbook is in
Chinese except for a Portuguese-Chinese street index. At the back there are appended
144 pages of advertisements. A 1978 edition also exists.

367 **Ou Mun kêng châi nin kám.** (Aòmén jīngjì niánjiàn.) (Almanac of
Macau's economy 1984-1986.)
Edited by Wong Hón-Keung (Huáng Hànqiáng) et al. Macau: Wá
K'iu Pou, 1986. 800p. map.

First published in 1983, this detailed directory in Chinese is composed of descriptive
chapters and lists of companies and institutions. Includes entries for industry, imports
and exports, real estate and construction, tourism, agriculture and fishing, commerce,
transport, water and electricity, finance, and life of the residents. Included are many

Directories

colour plates showing landscape and factory conditions in Macau. There are also aerial photographs and a considerable number of advertisements. An English version, is published under the title *Economy of Macau* (q.v.).

Anuário católico do ultramar português: Annuaire catholique de l' outre-mer portugais. (The Catholic yearbook of Portuguese overseas territories.) *See* item no. 188

Economy of Macau.
see item no. 235.

Bibliographies

368 **Exposição bibliográfica: P.^{e} Manuel Teixeira.** (Bibliographic exposition: Father Manuel Teixeira.)
Jorge de Abreu Arrimar, translated into Chinese by Wong Wai, translated into English by Maria do Rosário Pereira.   Macau: Direcção dos Serviços de Educação Biblioteca do Complexo Escolar, 1986. 27p. bibliog.
A thirteen page introduction to the life of Manuel Teixeira, Macau's most famous living resident historian, is followed by a list of 123 publications by the priest.

369 **Algumas notas sôbre a bibliografia de Macau.** (Some bibliographical notes on Macau.)
Charles Ralph Boxer, José Maria Braga.   Macau: Escola Tipográfica Salesiana, 1939. 30p.
Contains lists of manuscripts from the Biblioteca da Ajuda and the Biblioteca Nacional in Lisbon. Works from the Biblioteca Pública de Évora and the Arquivo Distrital de Évora also feature, while other texts cited come from the collections of the Jesuítas na Ásia and the Rerum Lusitanicarum. The introduction refers to a more detailed bibliography of the Jesuítas na Ásia Collection written in Japanese by Okamoto Ryōchi, *Porutogaru o tazuneru* (A Vist to Portugal), (1930).

370 **Bibliografia macaense.** (Macaense bibliography.)
Compiled by Luís Gonzaga Gomes, introduced by Jorge de Abreu Arrimar.   Macau: Instituto Cultural, 1987. 2nd ed. 202p.
Also published in the *Boletim do Instituto Luís de Camões*, vol. 7, no. 1, this bibliography contains over 1,800 items, mostly in Portuguese, listed by author and indexed in the general section. There are also sections on local legislation and periodicals. No annotations are provided.

Bibliographies

371   **A biblioteca do Capitão C. R. Boxer.** (The library of Captain Charles Ralph Boxer.)
José Maria Braga.   Macau: Escola Tipográfica do Orfanato, 1938. 14p.

Also published in the *Boletim Eclesiastico de Macau*, this article includes a list of publications by the Portuguese colonial historian, Charles Ralph Boxer, covering the years 1926-38. The preface discusses the 'Bibliotheca Boxeriana' by Boxer, and mentions some of the more famous works in the collection.

372   **Catálogo do manuscripts de Macau.** (Catalogue of manuscripts of Macau.)
Compiled by the Centro de Estudos Históricos Ultramarinos. Lisbon: The Author, 1960. 713p.

First published by the *Boletim da Filmoteca Ultramarina Portuguesa*, no. 19, the catalogue lists documents found in collections in Macau. Manuscripts are arranged within collections in chronological order with the earliest documents dating from 1611 and the latest dated 1899. An index of names, places and subjects is provided.

373   **Catálogo dos manuscritos de Macau.** (Catalogue of manuscripts of Macau.)
Compiled by Luís Gonzaga Gomes.   Lisbon: Centro de Estudos Históricos Ultramarinos, 1965. 147p.

Published as an off-print from no. 31 of the *Boletim da Filmoteca Ultramarina Portuguesa*, this catalogue comprises a list of government documents belonging to the civil administrative department during the years 1912-14. These documents were held in the library of the Leal Senado of Macau. The processing number, date, and a short description are given for each document.

374   **The Portuguese in Asia and the Far East: the Braga Collection in the National Library of Australia.**
Pauline Haldane.   In: *I.C.I.O.S. II – second international conference on Indian Ocean studies held at Perth, Western Australia, 5-12 December 1984.* Perth, Australia: University of Western Australia, Western Australian Institute of Technology, Western Australian College of Advanced Education, Murdoch University, 1984. 67p.

Includes a seven-page introduction to the life of José Maria Braga and to his book collection purchased by the National Library of Australia in 1966. Macau figures prominently in the Braga Collection which also includes books on other parts of East Asia (particularly Hong Kong and China), and on the Portuguese voyages with emphasis on the maps and nautical charts which the navigators produced. Appendices list books by Braga, rare books in the collection, material on World War II, 198 manuscript materials, 160 of the 1000 pictures in the collection (annotated by Braga), newspapers and newspaper clippings, and major serials.

375 **Portugal e a China: cinco séculos de relacionamento.** (Portugal and China: five centuries of relations.)
Compiled by the Ministério da Cultura. Lisbon: Biblioteca Nacional, 1984. 54p.

A preliminary bibliography with an initial print-run of only 350 copies covering manuscripts, monographs, and periodical publications on Luso-Chinese relations. The texts are largely, but not exclusively in Portuguese. This work, which is to be the basis for a larger bibliography on Portugal in East Asia, contains 254 entries from the Biblioteca Nacional in Lisbon, the Biblioteca da Ajuda in Lisbon and the collection of Dr. Carlos Estorninho. Works on Macau figure prominently.

376 **The Portuguese in Asia: an annotated bibliography of studies on Portuguese colonial history in Asia, 1498-c.1800.**
Compiled by Daya de Silva. Zug, Switzerland: IDC, 1987. 313p.

The emphasis is on primary sources, although secondary scholarly sources are also included. The 2,773 entries are divided into cartography, navigation, travel, conquest, religion, economy and the impact of Asian society. References to Macau are found in the East Asia sub-heading within these categories. Not all items are annotated.

377 **Exposição bibliográfica e documental.** (A bibliographic and documentary exhibition.)
Macau: Direcção dos Serviços de Educcação e Cultura, 1985. [18p.]

Provides an annotated catalogue of material found in the Biblioteca Nacional and the Arquivo Histórico which was displayed when President Eanes visited Macau in 1985.

378 **Luís Gonzaga Gomes photobibliographical exhibition: Luís Gonzaga Gomes exposição fotobibliográfica.**
Macau: Instituto Cultural, 1987. 86p.

A thirty-seven page, illustrated introduction to the life of this famous Macaense bibliographer and museum curator is followed by a complete bibliography of his works (p. 39-83). The introduction is in English, Portuguese and Chinese.

379 **De Portugal ao Extremo Oriente, exposição bibliográfica.** (From Portugal to the Far East, a bibliographic exhibition.)
Macau: Instituto Cultural, 1986. [40p.]

This catalogue was produced to accompany an exhibition of books from the Biblioteca Nacional and the Arquivo Histórico held in the Leal Senado building in 1986. The entries are in Portuguese and Chinese.

380   **Portugal / China 450 anos, exposição bibliográfica.** (Portugal / China 450
       years, a bibliographic exhibition.)
       Macau: Instituto Cultural, Arquivo Histórico, Biblioteca Nacional,
       1987. [40p.]
An annotated catalogue of books and curiosities published to accompany a
bibliographic exhibition held in Macau during April 1987. Photographs of old
manuscripts and the title pages from some books are reproduced. The titles and
notations are in Portuguese and Chinese. Most of the books listed are directly relevant
to Macau.

381   **Portugal e os descobrimentos, exposição bibliográfica.** (Portugal and the
       age of discoveries, a bibliographic exhibition.)
       Introduced by Antonío Martins Soares.   Macau: Instituto Cultural,
       Serviços de Marinha, Biblioteca Nacional, 1987. [48p.]
Documents the manuscripts displayed in Macau during July 1987 for an exhibition on
the Portuguese age of discovery. Annotations are in Portuguese and Chinese.

Boletim Bibliográficó de Macau. (Bibliographical Bulletin of Macau.)
See item no. 356.

Documentos sobre a história da China. (Documents on Chinese history.)
See item no. 332.

Index

The index is a single alphabetical sequence of authors (personal and corporate), titles of publications and subjects. Index entries refer both to the main items and to other works mentioned in the note to each item. Title entries are in italics. Numeration refers to the items as numbered rather than to page numbers.
Portuguese names are listed by the last part of the surname. Chinese and Japanese names are listed surname first without a comma, unless the author has adopted Western name order.

105

Map of Macau

This map shows the more important features and landmarks.

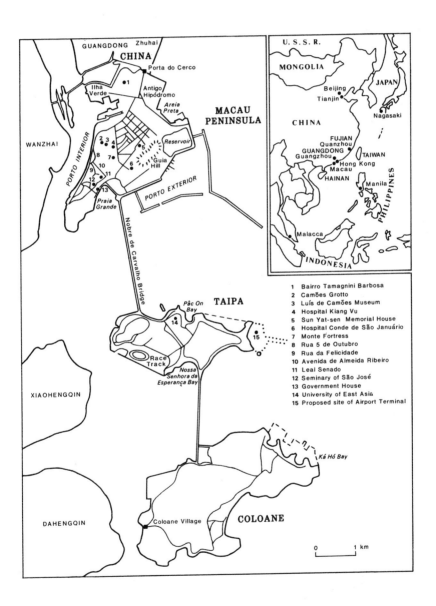

1 Bairro Tamagnini Barbosa
2 Camões Grotto
3 Luís de Camões Museum
4 Hospital Kiang Vu
5 Sun Yat-sen Memorial House
6 Hospital Conde de São Januário
7 Monte Fortress
8 Rua 5 de Outubro
9 Rua da Felicidade
10 Avenida de Almeida Ribeiro
11 Leal Senado
12 Seminary of São José
13 Government House
14 University of East Asia
15 Proposed site of Airport Terminal

13/9/89